"For over four years, I've observed Sage demonstrate her love for God and others as her pastor. Sage has a passion to communicate God's Word and His love with others. It's also clear that God has blessed her with a gift to convey stories through different mediums and with clarity. As you travel through familiar passages from the Bible, Sage will awaken your senses and help you see events from different angles. You will be blessed and your hunger for the Bible will only increase with every page turned. Enjoy the journey!"

— Todd Peters,
Pastor and Retired Navy SEAL

"Sage is a godly woman who loves the Lord passionately. Her heart will come through in this book and I fully expect readers to be blessed by what they read."

— Rev. Dale Sutherland,
President of USA Ministries for
International Care Ministries

"Stories hold a unique power to transform our lives. Sage McCullough has given her life to telling stories on the stage, and she brings her unique perspective and experience as a storyteller to *Last Adam*. Sage's book will help you experience these biblical stories in fresh and unexpected ways!"

— Kevin Cloud,
author of *God and Hamilton:*
Spiritual Themes From the Life of Alexander Hamilton
& the Broadway Musical He Inspired

"Sage McCullough's use of spirited imagination to see these ancient stories in fresh ways is a delight. As I read them, I was reminded of the creativity of William Young's *The Shack*, St. Ignatius's approach to encountering Scripture, and the theologians of the early church making surprising connections in the biblical story of God's work of healing and redemption. While not all readers will always agree on her interpretations in her storytelling, the book is an engaging, thoughtful, faithful, and delightful trip."

— Dr. David M. Hindman,
campus minister and pastor at The College of William
and Mary, and former pastor at Duncan Memorial United
Methodist Church on the campus of Randolph-Macon College

"There are a few books in my library that I read again and again... they are *Hammer of God, God's Smuggler, Born Again,* and George Whitefield's biography by Dallimore. *Last Adam* will be one of those books that help me see God's grace in a different way, and that I want to continually revisit... it is the 'grown up' version of the Jesus Storybook Bible... because of how it shows the gospel and the love of God in every story."

— Chris Gray,
Church Group Leader and
Former Men's Ministry Coordinator

"As I read this book, it was like I was meeting someone I had known my whole life for the first time again. Stories from the Scriptures that I knew since my childhood—I saw them again through a different set of eyes. The change of angle illuminated so many nuances of the stories, and brought such fresh perspectives. *Last Adam* felt like an insider's view of a story that I had known from a distance. There were so many things that spoke to me, and as I finished one chapter I wanted to jump into the next. Readers are going to love *Last Adam*!"

— Wesley Johnson,
Lead Pastor at First Assembly of God

"McCullough offers a fresh telling of some of our oldest stories in these poignant vignettes. Vivid imagery interwoven with the original source text, exquisitely rendered."

— Kenneth Corbin,
Independent Journalist and Editor

"Last Adam is a unique manuscript... beautifully written, with evocative imagery and theological depth. The material is insightful and will help readers consider familiar stories in a new way."

— Writer's Edge

LAST
ADAM

STORIES OF LOVE'S REDEMPTIVE POWER

BY

SAGE C. MCCULLOUGH

Published by Deep River Books
Sisters, Oregon
www.deepriverbooks.com

ISBN – 13: 9781632695802
Library of Congress Control Number: 2022900853

Headshot Photography by Brooke Avery of Avery Elizabeth Photography. www.averyelizabethphoto.com

Cover Design by Connie Gabbert

Printed in the USA

Sage C. McCullough
www.thedoyenne.net

For Colton

Love at First Breath

The Creator's breath
As soft as a whisper; it begins to mold.
Molding everything you are.
Your beginning starts from His love.

He wants you,
So much that He creates a world for you.
A world of abundant wonder for you.
He creates it from His love.

If you knew how the story would end, would you go on?
Would His love and Spirit be enough?
Would you trust in His plan?
Could you stop asking why long enough,
To allow Him to hold you through the pain?
Could you trust in His breath?

His breath that fills your lungs with grace and hope.
His breath that gives you the strength to carry on.
His breath that gives your faith peace.

His love comes at first breath

TABLE OF CONTENTS

- A reimagined account of creation through the eyes of the Trinity, focusing on the fact that God created Adam and Eve, knowing His children will betray His love. The story illustrates the roles of Jesus and the Holy Spirit at creation.

- A story to explain the fall of Lucifer, and how he challenges God, threatening to steal God's children away from Him.

- A retelling of the fall of Adam and Eve, and how God's love covers them with clothing.

- The story of Cain and Abel from Eve's perspective; concentrating on the mother's grief and guilt for her child's sin.

- This is a companion story to the first Love's Chosen. This is the story of Mary's life from the birth of Christ to her witness of His death on the cross.

- A passionate tale of the three hours of darkness while Jesus was on the cross.

- The story of doubting Thomas, explaining how Jesus uses his doubts to confirm His glory.

- The story of two stonings: Stephen's and Paul's. It is revealed that Paul's thorn is his memory of Stephen, and his guilt at being Saul.

- The story of John writing Revelation from a prison island.

- A modern story of a son on his death bed, illuminating how God uses all of the stories of the Bible to save him.

ACKNOWLEDGMENTS

There is no one greater to thank or honor for this book other than God. This is His love story, and I am so grateful to be a part of it, as His child. I would like to humbly thank the Holy Spirit for giving me the words to write this book and for sitting next to me while I typed.

God provided a blessing to me throughout this writing process: my husband, Brandon. All that I am, and anything I accomplish is because of him. Brandon's love creates an environment where success is possible. I want to also thank my children: Grace and Abel. They are what make me special, and being their mom is the greatest joy of my life. I am honored to be their wife and mother! I am so proud to be a part of Team Costanzo!

I would also like to thank my family for always supporting and loving me. They are the reason I know Jesus, and they have helped shape me into the woman I am today. I am so grateful for that gift of discipleship, and nothing could have been a greater act of love in my life. I thank all of you for always fostering and encouraging my relationship with God. To my sister and brother-in-law: Sara and Jeremy, you planted the seed for this book eighteen years ago. I want to thank you for helping me to realize God's calling. To Cortney, Cylie, Avery, Nathan, Elias, Kai, and Judah—I love you!

I would like to thank Elizabeth Lively for editing this book during its infancy. Your first edits shaped what this book is today. I would also like to thank Chris Gray. You read the book when no one else would, and your feedback energized me when I was feeling empty. I want to thank Ron and Carol Bowen, Todd Peters, Dale Sutherland, David Hindman, Wesley Johnson, Kenneth Corbin, and Kevin Cloud for supporting this endeavor.

A very big thank you to Andy Carmichael at Deep River Books (DRB). He not only believed in this book, but also in me. Andy's guidance, character, and professionalism have made this experience a pleasure. The friendship I have felt from DRB has encouraged me, and has felt like an answer from God. Tamara Barnet, thank you for guiding me through this process. I'm so grateful for the trajectory you created for this book. To my editor, Carolyn Currey, I cannot thank you enough for all you have done! You challenged and led me with respect and grace. You were dedicated to this story, and I appreciate all of the attention to detail you gave the manuscript.

This book is for my nephew Colton. You are ever present in my heart and thoughts, still inspiring me, and inspiring so much of this book. You are an example of God's breath, plan, and love. I miss you.

AUTHOR'S NOTE

Growing up, I always wondered... how could God ask Abraham to sacrifice his son? It seemed so extreme and lacked the love I was told God had for His children. I could never understand what purpose that sacrifice would have for God's kingdom. I could never reconcile why He allowed His children, past and present, to experience so much pain.

Eighteen years ago, I wrote a story for a Sunday School class, and in that moment *Last Adam* was born. God told me that my tiny story was part of a bigger story to answer my question about Abraham. So many feel the Bible is irrelevant, inaccessible, or contradictory. This causes people to view God as a supernatural being unleashing pain without love onto His children. *Last Adam* re-imagines moments of the Bible and connects them to our modern trials by expanding the brief verses into a larger picture of love, restoration, and rescue.

In 1 Corinthians 15, Paul writes a letter sharing the "good news" that reflects God's entire plan from Adam to Jesus. God breathed life into Adam, connecting the spirit and body, creating a soul. When sin entered the garden, the spirit that God breathed died, and man's soul lost contact with heaven. But the Trinity has been here since creation with a plan of love to connect our souls again to heaven. First Corinthians 15:45 promises that with Jesus all our lost traveling will end, because He is the "life-giving Spirit" to connect our souls again. Every one of us has been born from Adam. Jesus is the Last Adam, the final word.

Last Adam reflects God's truth within fictional narratives, assuring us that our trust in the Lord's love is justified. Ultimately, Last Adam is a love letter I wrote to honor God. This book is not meant to be a study guide, educational tool, or sermon; it is a story I want to share with you, the reader. Discover with me God's love and restoration in the midst of trials, confusion, and pain throughout the Bible.

LOVE AT FIRST BREATH

And the Lord God formed man of the dust of the ground and breathed into his nostrils the breath of life; and man became a living being.

Genesis 2:7

The God who made the world and everything in it is the Lord of heaven and earth, and does not live in temples built by human hands. And he is not served by human hands, as if he needed anything. Rather, he, himself gives everyone life and breath and everything else.

Act 17:24-25

In the beginning was the Word, and the Word was with God, and the Word was God. He was with God in the beginning. Through him all things were made; without him nothing was made that has been made. In him was life, and that life was the light of all mankind.

John 1:1-4

You are worthy, our Lord and God, to receive glory and honor and power, for you created all things, and by your will they were created and have their being.

Revelation 4:11

Mud and earth begin to fill the cracks and lines of His hands, but He continues to mold with a sober purpose. His mission is to complete creation. The mud starts to move up His forearms and He looks to His Father.

"Abba, guide My hands, help Me to create a masterpiece."[1]

He molds and molds with great precision, not allowing for any faults. He forms and forges, breathing in this birth of new life into His soul. It is left to the Son to create the child. This creation is a part of Him; the child is His purpose. It has to be the Son's love that molds the children, for it will be His love that saves them. The Father and Spirit are there with Him.

The Father's plan has always been... He encourages His Son, "My goal is that they will be encouraged and knit together by strong ties of love. I want them to have full confidence because they have complete understanding of My secret plan..." the Father bends down and joins the Son, "which is Christ... Yourself."[2]

Elohim only knows love; He is love.[3] A supernatural being beyond any comprehension, with cosmic fundamental and distinctive characteristics that can never be changed, and only classified as love. This creation will be the object of that love. The children are created in His image, allowing the Father to love them fully. They will fellowship together, and His children will bring Him joy. He does not need the children—the Three are complete—He just wants the children. He wants to be their Father. He wants to hold them, He wants to be close to them, and He wants to shower His love on them. The purpose of Elohim's love is to give it all to His children. That is what will bring Him complete joy. All He has created is for them...

Elohim spoke, and a home was made. Elohim spoke, and His light came so the darkness could have promise. Elohim spoke, and

---

[1] Abba means Daddy.
[2] Colossians 2:2 NLT
[3] Elohim means God the Creator.

created a waterfall, bursting forth to quench all of His children's thirsts. Elohim spoke, and created the sky to hold all of their dreams. Elohim spoke, and created land to give them a foundation for their purpose. He created mountains to give them a place to rise up. He created the valleys to give them a place of rest. Elohim spoke, and created the sun, giving it the fire to sustain life. Elohim spoke, and created the moon to shine security through the darkness. He created the stars sprinkled throughout the sky for them to make wishes on. He created time, slow and steady, for them to experience moments and chronicle memories. He created the birds to fly in the sky to give them inspiration, the fish of the sea to give them wisdom, and animals to give them comfort. Then Elohim blew His breath over all of it to bring it to life. His creation was good. Now it is time for the creation to become complete; His children need to be created. The Father has filled the earth with all of His blessings for His children. He did all of this because the plan is to love them, even though He knows His children will reject all of it. They will reject Him. All of creation will fall to its ruin. The sweet smell of it will turn sour, but the plan will hold steady. Elohim looks to His Son—the plan has always been...

The mud is drying onto the Son's hands now; tight and strained, it constricts His every movement. The labor of creating causes throbbing pain in the Son's arms. The Son feels a piercing pain in His hands. Sharp as a nail, but He forges on molding and shaping; His muscles ache with the weight of carrying this love on His back. The burden is heavy, but He forges on molding and shaping. His side aches, like a dagger through His lungs, but He forges on molding and shaping. His head is pounding; like hundreds of needles piercing His thoughts, but He forges on molding and shaping. He knows the truth, but He works on. He sighs deeply and whispers,

"*You* will lie to Me. *You* will deny Me. *You* will turn your back against Me."

He molds.

"*You* will use My name in vain to curse Me. *You* will be your greatest love, not Me. *You* will forget Me."

He molds.

"*You* will charge Me with blame. *You* will reject My word. *You* will destroy Me."

He molds.

"*You* will be the whip that licks My back. *You* will be the cross that I carry. *You* will be the thorn that crowns My head."

He molds.

"*You* will be the sword that pierces My side. *You* will be the nails that are driven into My hands and feet. *You* will be the sin I will die for."

He is finished.

The mud has created a callous cast around His hands and arms. A cast that He is too heartbroken to break through and will keep with Him forever. He sits there, looking at the nucleus of His creation, and He weeps. He weeps for all that is to come, for all of the choices the children will make. He weeps for the times when the children will feel unloved. He weeps for the times when the children will feel alone. He weeps for the times when the children will feel helpless. He cries out to His Father...

"Abba, show Me the way. Knowing all I have to sacrifice, it is still not yet enough, not for what will come upon them. This journey will be too difficult for them to bear; the suffering will be too great."

He weeps.

"My heart..." The Son cries out to His Father.

"My heart, Abba... My heart, it is filled with a deep love that pains Me to know their anguish. Lord, how will they ever know how much We love them?"

He weeps.

"How will they know that for every tear they shed, I will feel the nails, the crown, and bear the cross for an eternity, just to wipe that tear from their eyes? Abba, there has to be another way."

He weeps.

He looks down at His hands, and sees the dried, impenetrable, brown mud. His Father embraces Him; and He understands, for the Father is weeping too.

The Spirit comes, "See how very much our heavenly Father loves them, for He allows them to be called His children, and they really are..."[4] The Spirit holds them both. "Elohim's creation is very good.[5] His love will always be enough."

The Spirit tells the Father and Son that it is time. The Father takes His creation into His arms. Pride swells His heart as He looks down to His most beautiful creation. The Spirit enters the children and begins to fill their lungs with breath. The Father says...

"*You* will not understand. *You* will not know how *you* fit into Our eternal plan, but *you* do."

The Spirit exhales His breath...

"*You* will be My desire. *You* will be My call to glory."

The Spirit exhales His breath...

"*You* will be My greatest joy. *You* will be My greatest love."

The Spirit exhales His breath...

"*You* will be My essence. *You* will be My children."

The Father now breathes into the children's nostrils the life of His soul, and the children breathe out for the first time.

---

[4] 1 John 3:1 NLT
[5] Reference to Genesis 1:31.

LOVE'S BETRAYAL

You were in Eden, the garden of God... You were anointed as a guardian cherub, for so I ordained you. You were on the holy mount of God... You were blameless in your ways from the day you were created till wickedness was found in you... you were filled with violence, and you sinned. So I drove you in disgrace from the mount of God, and I expelled you, guardian cherub... Your heart became proud on account of your beauty, and you corrupted your wisdom because of your splendor. So, I threw you to the earth...

Ezekiel 28:13-17

How you are fallen from Heaven, O Lucifer, son of the morning! How are you cut down to the ground, you who weakened the nations! For you have said in your heart: I will ascend into heaven, I will exalt my throne above the stars of God; I will also sit on the mount of congregation on the farthest sides of the north; I will ascend above the heights of the clouds; I will be like the Most High.

Isaiah 14:12-14 NKJV

He replied, "I saw Satan fall like lightning from heaven."

Luke 10:18

For God did not spare even the angels who sinned. He threw them into hell, in gloomy pits of darkness, where they are being held until the day of judgment.

2 Peter 2.4 NLT

The one who does what is sinful is of the devil, because the devil has been sinning from the beginning. The reason the Son of God appeared was to destroy the devil's work.

1 John 3.8

He meets Him in the garden. The place that he is supposed to protect has now become the place of his judgment. Adonai called him to come; he does not have the power to refuse.[6]

"My Morning Star, I created you to be beautiful and perfect; now what have you done to yourself? Now your smell is repulsive."[7]

Lucifer does not speak. He has not been allowed yet. He must remain within Adonai's hold.

"Your pride has caused you to be blind. 'How you are fallen from Heaven, O Lucifer, son of the morning! How are you cut down to the ground...? For you have said in your heart: I will ascend into heaven; I will exalt my throne above the stars of God; I will also sit on the mount of congregation on the farthest sides of the north; I will ascend above the heights of the clouds; I will be like the Most High.'"[8]

Lucifer feels the rage throughout his being, but he is still confined. Adonai still holds him frozen in silence.

"You were created to have domain over My earth, to show them how to praise Yahweh.[9] I gave you My creation as a gift; you were a favored one. You were supposed to take this creation and lift everything

---

[6] Adonai means my master.
[7] Lucifer means Morning Star.
[8] Isaiah 14:12–14
[9] Yahweh means Self-Existent One.

high unto Me. Now what have you brought into my world? A putrid darkness."

Lucifer quivers from the Father's breath. Adonai pulls him close, so His breath is suffocating him.

"Hear Me now..."

Adonai feels Lucifer's trembling.

"Your choice makes you tremble. You wanted to be lifted up high above Me, but now that I have brought you to Me, you tremble at the separation you just caused."

Lucifer cannot breathe; Adonai's height is too high, but Adonai gives him what he asked for.

"Hear Me now, all of My creation hear me now... My Morning Star is no longer. I only see My enemy before Me. I sentence you to an eternity in a lake of fire, apart from Me. Your place will always be apart from Me. That will be your hell."

The echo of the Father's words cracks the earth, and creation has been forever changed. It is time. Even though He knows what is in his heart, Yahweh will allow him to speak. He releases Lucifer's confinement, and bile comes slithering out of his lips.

"Yes, You gave me life. You gave me a heavenly body full of strength and power.[10] I can hold the wind back with my hands.[11] I can command fire at my will.[12] I can calm nature with my call.[13] But still You wanted more; You made *man*. You made *him* in Your image... *not me, but him*. That inferior creature is who You crown with glory and honor.[14] *He* is the one You love. My hate and loathing for *him* is greater than any power You have given me. You gave *him* authority over the earth, and now I must see *him* in my place."

---

[10] Reference to Revelation 18:1.

[11] Reference to Revelation 7:1.

[12] Reference to Psalm 104:4.

[13] Reference to Psalm 148:1-4.

[14] Angels have superior wisdom: reference to Zechariah 1 & 6.

Lucifer laughs. A laugh that erupts all of his evil. Adonai crushes him down under His heel, but allows him to finish speaking.

"I will take him from You. I will tempt him. I will tempt them all. I will become the head of the human race; Your children will become mine. I will become their father. I have brought sin, and You cannot be with sin. They will choose *me* over You, and I will become the god of this world. I am the rightful ruler of Earth, and I will make Your *man* love *me* more."

The truth of Lucifer's words leaves a foul stench in the air, and the Father's heart becomes heavy. Yahweh looks to His Son and breathes in His Spirit. All has already been foreknown and foreordained. They understand what needs to happen. They know the battle plan. It was always about choice. His will can only be carried out through the choice of His children. Love always begins with choice. The children can choose light and life with the Father, or darkness and death with the Deceiver, but because He loves them, the Father will give them the choice. He could stop this now and start over, but that is force, not love. Love can only grow and thrive through choice. His voice bellows over Lucifer, and Lucifer trembles with fear. He does not understand the plan, but he knows his time is limited. Lucifer knows his life is and always will be in Adonai's hands.

"I will allow you to bring sin into this world. I will allow you to tempt and show My children the choices. I will rule by love and give My children freedom to choose you. But..." His voice commands all of nature: every animal falls to the ground, every tree bows in reverence, the mountains shake, and every living thing, including Lucifer, cowers before Him. "My Spirit will give them light in your darkness. My Son will give them truth when you tell lies. And I will be the promise they need. In the end, they will know I Am the only choice of love." He releases Lucifer, like flicking away the nuisance of a fly. Lucifer is released into the world, but God is in control.

LOVE'S COVERING

Now the serpent was more crafty than any of the wild animals the LORD God had made. He said to the woman, "Did God really say, 'You must not eat from any tree in the garden'?" The woman said to the serpent, "We may eat fruit from the trees in the garden, but God did say, 'You must not eat fruit from the tree that is in the middle of the garden, and you must not touch it, or you will die.'" "You will not certainly die," the serpent said to the woman. "For God knows that when you eat from it your eyes will be opened, and you will be like God, knowing good and evil." When the woman saw that the fruit of the tree was good for food and pleasing to the eye, and also desirable for gaining wisdom, she took some and ate it. She also gave some to her husband, who was with her, and he ate it. Then the eyes of both of them were opened, and they realized they were naked; so they sewed fig leaves together and made coverings for themselves. Then the man and his wife heard the sound of the Lord God as he was walking in the garden in the cool of the day, and they hid from the Lord... but the Lord God called to the man, "Where are you?" ... The Lord God made garments of skin for Adam and his wife, and clothed them.

Genesis 3:1-9, 21

The thief comes only to steal and kill and destroy. I came that they may have life and have it to the full.

John 10:10

Satan, who is the god of this evil world, has made him blind, unable to see the glorious light of the Gospel that is shining upon him or to understand the amazing message we preach about the glory of Christ, who is God.

2 Corinthians 4:4 TPB

The grass beneath His feet feels cool. The sun is beginning to take its rest and all is calm. Elohim created this meadow for their walks. He feels longing for it when He is not there, excited anticipation as He walks toward it, and at home when He enters. It is His favorite place in all of creation because it is their meeting place. Here Elohim sees His daughter, Eve, gently caress and care for the animals; watching her sweetness highlights the glory of His creation. Here He watches Adam investigate every trait of the animals to give them a fitting name. Great joy fills the Father's heart as Adam and Eve study and learn from Him. Here is where the Father's children make Him laugh as they discover something new. Here is where the Father's children make Him smile as He delights in their play. Here is where the Father's children make His love complete as they say "I love You, Abba."

They meet at the end of the day because the setting sun makes everything brilliant; everything the fading rays touch sparkles like diamonds. Elohim created this paradise for them to gather together. He placed flowers of every color throughout the garden, cascading over the meadow like a blanket. He made the grass soft and lush; it is the perfect cushion to the children's feet. He placed a waterfall at the center, gathering at the bottom to create a blue lagoon. Water so pure that it quenches the children's every thirst. This is the meadow where they take walks every day. Day after day, time is not counted here. In this meadow, the children only know joy and love. But... today... today, after so many days, the meadow is different. There is no home or world small enough that choice cannot enter. The supernatural protection of the garden is not to blockade choice from leaking through. Today, the Father knows the plan has to begin.

Today, He knows the beauty of His creation has changed. The utopia has metamorphosed; the essence has dulled and the purity is gone. The animals cry out in pain, the waters stop, the sun hides, and there is no breath in the air. A cancer has infected the garden and the children's souls, causing them to decay. Death has entered the garden, and the children understand it. A sadness enters the Father's heart. A sadness so deep and heavy, all of creation feels it and weeps with His broken heart. The children made a choice. The free gift of making a decision when faced with different possibilities is the gift God provided out of love. The children claim the choice of death instead of His love. Life has changed.

"Adam, where are you?"[15]

He knows their hiding place. He is disappointed they choose to hide. They do not understand His love. They are children, but they are His children, so He will call once more.

"Adam, where are you?"

Shame makes their feet heavy. Slowly they come from the shadows, embarrassed by their nakedness, embarrassed by their sin. There is a stigma now. The children no longer have His mark on them. The Father breathes them in. His creation's once sweet smell is now tainted. He can smell the Deceiver on them, and it stings His nostrils.[16] The children approach Him cautiously, never looking up to His face.

"I heard your voice in the garden, and I was afraid because I was naked; and I hid myself."[17] Adam can barely whisper through his shame.

"Who told you that you were naked?"[18]

There is a new understanding. The children can see themselves now with new eyes. Their bodies now shame them, causing a new feeling of modesty. The nakedness not only exposes their bodies, but

---

[15] Genesis 3:8
[16] Deceiver is another name for Satan.
[17] Genesis 3:10
[18] Genesis 3:11

their hearts as well. Hearts that once only belonged to the Father now have darkness in them. They are raw and nude. He looks down at their bodies and sees every cell, every hair, and every breath. The blueprint for their chemistry was so exact to every small detail. He exhausted all of His might making sure He created a masterpiece through His children that would glorify His image... and now, they are just naked.

His heart grieves for the closeness they once shared. Their quiet moments together will no longer be. Their walks and conversations, their time together spoiled by a desire for more than just Him. Now all is forever changed. As they reveal themselves to Him, He can see the regret in their hearts. It is pressing and binding, not allowing them to be close to Him. The sin awakened the knowledge of evil and brought pain into the world. The sin separates His children from Him. He cannot hold sin; He can no longer hold them. He will have to let go. The garden begins to crumble under the weight of the Father's tears.

The Father has to embrace them... He has to love them. He has to make things right. He needs to reconcile them. A substitute has to be made. He knows blood has to be shed. He has to give them covering, giving them a shield against the world. He needs to cover their nakedness. He sees their feeble attempt to make their own covering. Simple garments of leaves that cannot withstand the new burdens they will endure.

The Son picks the lamb. The best lamb, innocent and pure; the lamb the Father loves the most. It is pure white; the little lamb has known no sin. He takes the lamb into His arms and whispers into its ear that He is going to make everything good again. Then He cuts the lamb and lets the blood flow. He sheds its blood to cover His children in love. He takes the lamb's skin and uses it to cover their shame. He weaves the covering together with as much care as He fashioned them. They will feel no cold. They will feel no burn. They will feel no wind. They will feel no shame.

"I do this because I love you, and now, this is how you are to love Me. Choose Me. Choose My light, choose My love, and choose to follow Me. Now you have to make your own covering and shed the blood of the innocent for atonement until He comes and crushes the head of the serpent; shedding blood for the last time."[19]

The children bow in repentant humility to their Holy Father and ask for forgiveness. He instantly forgives with no hesitation and with no resentment—just with love. It is now time for them to leave. Not a punishment, but grace. It is the only way to hold His children once more.

"I cannot let you live forever in this sin; I need to hold you once more. I send you away so I can have you with Me always."[20] With tears flowing from the Father's eyes, He opens the gates of the garden; the Spirit leads the way and the children leave. "For you were made from the dust, and to the dust you will return."[21]

The plan begins.

---

[19] Reference to Genesis 3:15.
[20] Reference to Genesis 3:22-23.
[21] Genesis 3:19 NLT

LOVE'S GRIEF

In the course of time Cain brought some of the fruits of the soil as an offering to the Lord. And Abel also brought an offering—fat portions from some of the firstborn of his flock. The Lord looked with favor on Abel and his offering, but on Cain and his offering He did not look with favor. So, Cain was very angry, and his face was downcast. Then the Lord said to Cain, "Why are you angry? Why is your face downcast? If you do what is right, will you not be accepted? But if you do not do what is right, sin is crouching at your door; it desires to have you, but you must rule over it." Now Cain said to his brother Abel, "Let's go out to the field." While they were in the field, Cain attacked his brother Abel and killed him.

Genesis 4:3-8

Those along the path are the ones who hear, and then the devil comes and takes away the word from their hearts, so that they may not believe and be saved.

Luke 8:12

You belong to your father, the devil, and you want to carry out your father's desires. He was a murderer from the beginning, not holding to the truth, for there is no truth in him. When he lies, he speaks his native language, for he is a liar and the father of lies.

John 8:44

She hears the cry and comes running, just like when they were babies. But in her heart, she knows that this time a kiss on the cheek will not heal the wounds; she can sense the dread in the cry that fills the air. She is running so hard that she feels the ground breaking the skin beneath her feet. She knows she is almost there, but then Eve suddenly stops. Frozen, she doesn't want to know. She is too scared to see it. She knows in her heart it is going to be him. She knows in her heart something has happened that cannot be undone. She begins to shake, and screams out to her Father.

"Abba, come here now!"

Eve is paralyzed in fear. If she moves, she cannot stay in denial. Her scream becomes barely a whisper.

"Abba, help my feet to move and give me the strength to look upon him."

The Spirit comes and fills her lungs with breath, and she slowly moves her feet. She knows there is no need for urgency because he is already gone. She can feel it in her soul. In fear, Eve approaches and she sees his body. Then suddenly again the urgency comes, all of her fear is gone, and she runs to her baby boy.

His body lies still on the ground; the thick red blood has stained the green grass. Abel, long beyond the need of his mother, is an old man, but in his face she only sees her baby. She reaches to wipe the dirt and blood away that is beginning to harden into his wrinkles.[22] She looks down at the blood on her hands and quiet tears come. Her legs can no longer support her breaking heart, and she collapses next to him. The quiet tears quickly become a rage of raw emotions. Eve screams out in agony. She beats the ground beside Abel, trying to command it to stop this pain. Her screams pierce the Father's ears. She screams out all of her agony, distorting and wrenching her body, exhausting every muscle. She accuses Satan for the Devil he is. Eve knows the Deceiver took Cain and killed Abel.

---

[22] Theologians estimate that Abel was over one hundred years old at the time of the murder.

A new evil has entered the world. She has felt its presence for a while. It was not just one moment, but a growing disappointment. A seed of anger planted long ago that the Deceiver has been watering for years in Cain's heart. Eve has been trying for so long to be more powerful in Cain's life than the Deceiver. She has lost count of the years she has been praying for Abba's love to reach him.

She told Cain of all the moments Abba would hold her and talk with her about His plans for her. She told Cain of all of the moments when Abba would seek her out just to spend time with her. Abba would talk with her, and show her His creation that He made just for her. Abba would sit with Eve, and explain each star to her. Adam had the animals, but Abba gave her the stars. She told Cain of all the moments when Abba would love her like the perfect father He was. She tried to remind Cain that Abba loved him so much, but the Deceiver would always close his ears so he could not hear her. Over and over, Cain's anger won over his heart. The Deceiver won.

She knows in her mind what happened in this field today, but her heart cannot believe it. She cannot believe Abel is now here on the ground, by the hands of his brother. Her screaming exhausts her body and stillness intrudes on her. Numbing her tears and her voice, Eve wants the silence to numb her mind. But no matter the time or silence, a mother's heart does not numb. No matter how old they are or how far they move from her, they are her babies. They are no longer able to snuggle in her lap, but Cain and Abel are still her children, and she lost both of them on this field today. How quickly it happened. The morning light brought such promise, and now in the evening's twilight she has to face every single day in darkness without ever having the morning light again.

She tells herself to breathe, but her breath is caught on a sob. A sob she is scared to release. To release it would make all of this real. The Spirit comes to her. She is a child that needs her daddy at this moment.

"Daughter, your heart is in pain."

"Abba, I am not strong enough for this. It is too much for me..."

"I am here."

"Abba. What have I done?"

"Did your hands do this?"

"No... but I did this; I brought sin in."

"Choices can be a great burden. You made a choice, and now Cain made his."

"Was it his choice? It was my sin that created all of this; I caused him to be born in sin. I disobeyed first. Abba, first I failed You, and now I have failed my son. This is all on my hands; this is my murder. How can I live with myself?"

The Father's heart breaks because Eve has been living in the guilt of lies. His Spirit holds her tighter.

"No, daughter. After all of these years you are still listening to the lies of the Deceiver. It was not your sin, but the Devil's. He seduced you to a solitary place, away from Adam. The Devil separates: that is all he does. Separates you from Me. It was he who made Adam fall, and he lured mankind away from me. He brought sin, not you."

She wants to believe what her Abba is saying, but her regret has created a thick barrier around her heart. The Deceiver has never stopped telling her lies, and has held his grip of guilt on her for so long. She has put the world's darkness on her shoulders.

"Father, do You regret me?" Eve's voice becomes small. "Why me? Why was I the one you created?"

Her shame has even kept her from allowing Abba to love her completely. The Father is tired of it; He wants His daughter back. His beautiful, love-of-His-life daughter back.

"Oh, My precious daughter, My love for you is endless. I created you so I could have joy. No other daughter would do. It had to be you. When I look at you, I only see My beautiful daughter who I love. I covered your sin with the blood, it is gone, and I can no longer see it. We were one in the garden, and we will be one again. The Son will come and make it all good again."

"I do not deserve your forgiveness..."

"Children always deserve forgiveness when they ask. I forgave you and gave you children to love, so you could have a glimpse of what I feel for you. Come back to Me fully, and allow Me to heal you of all your pain."

"How can You heal this pain? It is too great."

"Nothing is too great for Me."

"But Abba..."

The Father knows everything that is in that rebuttal.

"Eve, nothing is too great for Me."

"Your mercy is too great."

"My mercy is for all of My children."

"Please have mercy on Cain. He took everything away; he took my Breath, but I still love him. He is still my child."[23]

"Cain is My child first, and I love him too. My love does not end with disobedience, nor when one stops loving me. But he ran away from Me and went to the darkness. How can light live in darkness? There is no darkness in Me; therefore, he is lying when he says he has fellowship with Me and yet goes on living in the darkness."[24]

She looks down again at the blood on her hands. Abel is no more. She has known for a long time that Cain's heart no longer belonged to the Father. She knew of his choice, but Eve did not know evil could end in this way. She did not understand how precious life is. Abel has no more life. That thought stops her heart. Abel is gone; she will not have him any longer. The waves of pain hit her again, and knock her down fully to the ground. She tastes Abel's blood on the grass. All is lost to her. The chaos is engulfing her mind with a throbbing ache. How can she ever be whole again? How can she find peace? How can she even move? A whirlwind of emotions keeps swirling around her. The Father hears all of these thoughts.

"Daughter, give me your guilt and broken heart. Allow Me to help you find peace. Allow Me to carry you."

---

[23] The name Abel means breath.

[24] Reference to 1 John 1:5-6.

Eve lifts her head and looks to Him desperately.

"Can you help me to understand this?"

"Daughter, his heart is living in darkness. You cannot see or understand the ways of darkness. In the garden I showed you sacrifice. I shed the blood of the innocent to forgive you, and that forgiveness clothed you. The blood of an innocent is the only sacrifice. That is the way I have commanded all of you to come to Me. It is only through repentance and blood that you can be My children. Cain chose to come to me with darkness in his heart disguised as fruit; an offering of sin, not obedience. I love Cain, and I asked him to come again. I warned him to respond correctly so sin could not enter. But the darkness kept him away, and suffocated him in sin."[25]

"I know. I have felt the darkness for a long time. I thought I could make it better. I thought my love for both of them would heal the wounds. I thought if I loved You enough, Cain would love You too."

"It is not your love that failed, but his. Abel loved purely, but Cain did not. Cain became Lucifer's child. 'How can goodness be a partner with wickedness...What harmony can there be between Christ and the Devil?'... My children are my living temple... I will be their God and they will be my people...Therefore, they cannot touch the filthy things of the Deceiver for Me to welcome them."[26] Eve feels hopeless, so the Spirit breathes out His grace. "But I will spare Cain out of mercy."[27]

Eve feels relief. She knows she has lost both of her sons on this field; her grief is for two, but the Father's mercy blesses her. The Spirit embraces her, and she finally releases her sob. She lets out her suffering. It is loud and deep, coming from a place of pain she never knew existed. She gives it all to her Father. There is nothing left to feel but the emptiness. She lost her children; there is no greater pain. The grief scares her because she knows it will be with her forever.

---

[25] Reference to Genesis 4:5-7.

[26] Reference to 2 Corinthians 6:14-18.

[27] Reference to Genesis 4:11-16.

"Do not fear the grief. I will be with you in it. I will love you through it."

Then suddenly Eve realizes she is not the only one grieving. She hears the grief in His voice too. He, too, has the mark of a grieving parent. Eve suddenly realizes how her Father felt that day in the garden. He, too, lost both of His children that day. He was never able to hold them again after that day, like she will never be able to hold Cain and Abel again. Years turned into decades, into centuries, and the Father is still waiting to hold His children. She is humbled with her new understanding.

"Abba..."

"Shh... I know..."

"I did not understand..."

"I know..."

Eve sits there in the knowledge that Abba knows the pain of her grieving heart better than anyone else. She feels remorse that she never once looked at things through His eyes to see the grief He has been carrying. Instead, Eve has selfishly enjoyed all the pleasures of His blessings on her life. She looks in Abel's face, and thousands of memories flood her mind at once.

"For so long I grieved leaving You in the garden. I thought I could never survive that grief. Then You blessed me with children, and I slowly forgot. I forgot about my life in the garden because my children made me feel full. At first, I felt ashamed of the happiness they gave me. I loved them so much, I was grateful to be out of the garden."

Eve looks to Abba, shocked that she let the words come out of her mouth.

"I could not believe that You would give me such a wonderful gift after my sin. My children were all I could see and love; I didn't long for the garden any longer. I am sorry if I loved them too much..."

The Father allows her to feel all Three of them, just like in the garden.

"The garden was never the plan. You and Adam were just the beginning... I needed you to be the mother. The mother of all people everywhere.[28] That is why I chose you, because you had the heart of a mother. Do not be sorry. Do not feel shame of the happiness your children gave you. It shows you the happiness you give Me."

The Spirit holds her, and His voice quiets her mind.[29]

"One day, I will feel happiness when My Son's blood is shed. Because in that day, His blood will cover My children, bring them back to Me, and I'll hold them forever."

Though she failed Him, in His great mercy, He still blessed her with children. Though she failed Him, He would heal her heart. And though she failed Him, He loved her. Eve understands His plan, and breathes the Spirit in. With her Abba holding her in His forgiving arms, they grieve together for the children they have lost. She sobs in His peace.

---

[28] Reference to Genesis 3:20.

[29] The Bible references over and over that the Holy Spirit came upon believers in the Old Testament for God's purposes. Judges 3:10, Judges 14:6, Judges 15:14, Nehemiah 9:30, Zechariah 4:6 are just a small few. Hebrews 11 speaks of many people from the Old Testament that had the Holy Spirit dwell within them.

LOVE'S COVENANT

Then the Lord saw that the wickedness of man was great in the earth,
and that every intent of the thoughts of his heart was only evil continually.
And the Lord was sorry that he had made man on the earth, and he was
grieved in his heart. So the Lord said, "I will destroy man whom I have
created from the face of the earth, both man and beast, creeping thing and
birds of the air, for I am sorry that I have made them."
But Noah found grace in the eyes of the Lord.

Genesis 6:5-8 KJV

The highest heavens belong to the Lord,
but the earth he has given to mankind.

Psalm 115:16

For from him and through him and for him are all things.
To him be the glory forever...

Romans 11:36

He looks down upon His creation and His heart grieves. He is filled with regret. He made no error in His creation, but there is a change. He now holds a deep sadness for the choices the children are making.

Adam's children have chosen to follow the Deceiver, and only one of Seth's descendants remain: Noah.[30] The Deceiver introduces death to the children, and he takes away their innocence and replaces it with agony and suffering. The children rejoice in the lies and sing praises to the evil. Only the Lord repents for their sins.[31] Only the Lord's heart breaks. To preserve His plan, the Lord has to take it all away. He has to atone for the death; He has to resolve it, or there will be nothing left. The Lord loves Noah more than His creation and He is willing to make the sacrifice.

Noah—the only one left that still calls Him Abba. His beautiful son is the only child left in all of this misery. All the others are the Deceiver's children. The Father will rescue His last child. A new creation will be made, and the plan will continue on.

Broken from hopelessness, Noah looks at his crops and sees the vines are no longer bearing fruit. He looks across the land, and sees no fruit anywhere. Others scoff at his crops, and tell him that the world has more control than Yahweh. Noah is hopeless for the crops, he is hopeless for the people, but as he holds his dead fruit in his hands he looks up.

"I have hope in You."

The Spirit approaches Noah softly in a whisper.

"You have found favor with Yahweh; you are His child that He loves."[32]

The Spirit feels the trouble in Noah's heart. Noah has been grieving endlessly for the world of his forefathers. He does not recognize the land in which he lives any longer. All have forgotten the Father, and he has not known peace for so long.

---

[30] Noah is a descendant of Seth.

[31] The Hebrew word used to describe God's repentance is *nacham* and it means "to be moved to pity." Therefore, it is not implying that God has made a mistake or changed His mind, but He is making a judgment based on others' decisions.

[32] Reference to Genesis 6:8.

"Noah, take My breath, breathe Me in, and know My peace. I have to come to rescue you. The Father's tears will come to wash the earth clean. Clean and beautiful again."

"El Shaddai, I only live to serve You."[33]

"Yes, you do live to serve Me and you are blameless. Like your fathers before you, you share My heart. I will not let you drown with the wicked. I will provide a salvation from judgment."

"Tell me what I must do, and I will give You my all."

"I am going to put an end to all people, for the earth is filled with disgust because of them. I am surely going to destroy both them and the earth. It is no longer My creation. The Deceiver has ravaged it; swallowing it whole, and then vomiting it back; putrefied and decayed..." The Spirit whispers... "But wait to see the glory that will come... wait to see the power that will come... wait to see the love that will come to protect you."

Noah's mind is racing, but his heart is still as the Spirit continues.

"So make yourself an ark of cypress wood; make rooms in it and coat it with pitch inside and out. This is how you are to build it: The ark is to be three hundred cubits long, fifty cubits wide and thirty cubits high. Make a roof for it, leaving below the roof an opening one cubit high all around. Put a door in the side of the ark and make lower, middle, and upper decks. I am going to bring floodwaters on the earth to destroy all life under the heavens, every creature that has the breath of life in it. Everything on earth will perish. But I will establish my covenant with you, and you will enter the ark—you and your sons and your wife and your sons' wives with you. You are to bring into the ark two of all living creatures, male and female, to keep them alive with you. Two of every kind of bird, of every kind of animal, and of every kind of creature that moves along the ground will come to you to be kept alive. You are to take every kind of food that is to be eaten and store it away as food for you and for them."[34]

---

[33] El Shaddai means God Almighty.
[34] Genesis 6:14–21

The Spirit looks into Noah's heart and sees his fear. He must comfort His son.

"Elohim, fear is possessing my heart; this task is too great for me. The size is too big; the burden will kill me. Is there no one else to stand beside me; no one to bring me comfort? My ancestors called you Abba. I am a patriarch of your creation, and yet I am alone. Can you not spare just one to help me?"

"You are not alone; I am with you. I will be your comfort. Your hands will be My hands, and I will build this ark for you. You are the only one left who honors Me. Your ancestors of Cain chose to walk away from My path. He did not want to be his brother's keeper or My son.[35] Abel's blood cries out to Me from the ground, but Cain cursed him.[36] He cursed all of his children. Look what the sins of the father can do.[37] But still I loved him and spared him from vengeance; I marked him as mine and granted him mercy to live in Nod.[38] Now that mercy has been in vain; for his children have destroyed My earth and know Me no longer. So I waited… I waited for thousands of years for you. Your father, Lamech, named you Noah for he said, 'He will comfort us in the labor and painful toil of our hands caused by the ground the Lord has cursed.'[39] You are the comfort and rest—you are Noah.[40] You will be the comfort from the sin. You will bring the rest from My judgment. You will be the preacher of righteousness."[41]

"How can I be a part of Your plan?"

"You will build My *ta-va*; the ark of My salvation.[42] It will be a glorious vessel of preservation, not destruction. You will build only one

---

[35] Reference to Genesis 4:9.

[36] Reference to Genesis 4:10.

[37] Reference to Deuteronomy 5:9.

[38] Reference to Genesis 4:13-16.

[39] Genesis 5:28-29

[40] Noah means "comfort or rest."

[41] Reference to 2 Peter 2:5.

[42] *Ta-va* is Hebrew for ark. It is only used twice in the Bible: here, and to describe Moses' basket.

door; only one way to enter. There will always only be one way to enter into my kingdom.[43] I will be on the other side of the door with you. Those who enter will receive salvation; those who stay in the world will receive death. This has been My plan from the beginning. Noah, you have been My plan from the beginning."

"Why me? Who am I to serve in Your glory?"

"You are My son. A most beloved son with whom I have found favor. I love all of My children; it grieves My heart that they choose to walk away from Me. My heart breaks to see their revolt with the darkness. Now only yours is what is left of Seth's pure blood for My light to enter into this world. If this is not done, then death will come and destroy My plan. I have to rescue you. I would gladly give up My creation to rescue just one of My lost sheep."

"All of this is for me? For my rescue?"

"My love is too great to let the darkness swallow you. You will bring My glory back to the world. Everything from the whispers of the wind to the roaring of the sea is to glorify Me. Even the Dark One exists to bring glory to Me. Now you, too, will glorify Me. You will build the ark of My glory."

"My Father, I will do as You have instructed."

"My Spirit will be with you. I will provide all you need. The floods will not overwhelm you, no matter how hard the boat will rock you. You will be the paradigm for the leader that is to come. You are the righteous one that will be spared from the wicked waters, so you can prepare the way for the One who will spare the wicked from sinking in the waters of death forever. You will survive the flood because of the shelter of the ark, so someday the One to come can be the shelter for all creation. You will emerge from the flood to a new creation, and I will create a covenant with you, so you can prepare a way for the Light

---

[43] Reference to Jesus being the only way to salvation. Like the ark, there is only ever one door to God.

that will enter the world to pierce the darkness.[44] The Light will enter so the children will never be in darkness again. The One will emerge as a new creation as well, but His covenant will bring everlasting peace and life. This is not sin's ultimate punishment—that will fall to the One on the cross. This is a rescue mission."

Noah obeys and begins to build. For 120 years he builds. It takes 120 years for this rescue mission to develop correctly. It takes 120 years for God to build the perfect vessel. One hundred and twenty years, waiting for the salvation to come. Knowing the plan does not make the time go faster for Noah. For 120 years, the Holy Spirit tells him "not yet" every time Noah cries out. Every time he is tired, every time he is discouraged, and every time he feels alone, the Holy Spirit comes. Noah cannot always feel it; sometimes the calluses on his hands and body ache too much from the labor. Sometimes the exhaustion overtakes his will and motivation. Sometimes the constant mockery of the world is too much for him. But for 120 years, the Holy Spirit puts strength into Noah's hands. For 120 years, the Holy Spirit renews his soul. For 120 years, the Holy Spirit quiets the noise of others. For 120 years, the Holy Spirit helps Noah craft the ta-va. For 120 years, the Holy Spirit gives him grace to wake up each day, breathe, and carry on. For 120 years the Holy Spirit keeps His promises to His child until the ark is finished.

The years have given Noah the time to ask every question. From questions that annoy his practicality like, "How can I feed so many animals?" to questions that torture his soul like, "Why did you allow Satan to have so much control?" Each question left him wondering how he will survive this calling, and did not answer the biggest question of them all: "Why me?" The questions do not stop the floods from coming. Water comes from every direction... plummeting hard from above disintegrating hope... colliding from the east and west, at once

---

[44] God gives Noah a rainbow as a seal of His covenant with him.

shattering peace... smashing from below, collapsing trust. God shuts the door and waits for the storms to stop.

The ark is three hundred cubits long, fifty cubits wide, and thirty cubits high. Noah trusts his Father built the right-sized boat to float above the storm. Noah knows it takes a boat this large to hold the Lord's covenant. It is a colossal boat that ultimately crashes into a mountain when the storm stops. After 120 years of Noah questioning, "Why me," God gives him the answer there on the mountain as he looks to the ark. The ark looks small to Noah as the animals leave it peacefully. The ark has served its purpose, and brought Noah to the place God wants him to be. It is time to stop counting the time and trust the answers to the questions, because the Father is good and has a plan. Noah walks away from the ark, and leaves it on the side of the mountain top. Noah looks to the sky and sees God's gift for him. The Father's light enters the tears that flooded the earth. Striking the water, reflecting the goodness of each droplet, separating out the darkness to showcase the Father's rainbow of love. Noah looks out to this new world, remembering the Spirit's words, and sees how God's love did protect, bring power, and reveal His glory. After 120 years, Noah no longer feels alone.

LOVE'S BALLAD

Then the Lord said to Satan, "Have you considered my servant Job, that there is none like him on the earth, a blameless and upright man, one who fears God and shuns evil? And still he holds fast to his integrity, although you incited me against him, to destroy him without cause."

Job 2:3

I have no peace; no quietness; I have no rest, but only my turmoil.

Job 3:26

Be merciful to me, Lord, for I am faint; O Lord, heal me, for my bones are in agony, my soul is in anguish. How long, O Lord, how long?

Psalm 6:2-3

I am worn out from sobbing. All night I flood my bed with weeping, drenching it with my tears.

Psalm 6:6 NLT

Consider it pure joy, my brothers and sisters, whenever you face trials of many kinds, because you know that the testing of your faith produces perseverance.

*Let perseverance finish its work so that you may be mature and complete, not
lacking anything*

James 1:2-4

Job cannot even sit; he is too broken. He gathers what is left of his
soul into a heap on the floor. He is too exhausted to even cry out
in his pain. The Accuser has had his way with Job, and there is nothing
left.[45] He can feel the presence of the Accuser surrounding him, like
a serpent squeezing its prey to death. Job has asked both the Accuser
and the Lord, over and over again why this is happening. Job has done
nothing but serve his Yahweh faithfully with all of himself. But Job
continues to lose everything again and again, and he continues to wait
to hear from the Lord. Instead, all he hears are the lies from the Accuser
that slither into his ears...

"Adonai is gone; like everything else..."

All Job has left to give the Lord are his tears; they are his only words
now. His tears from a pain he can no longer bear. All has been lost, all
has been destroyed, and he no longer knows how to survive this world
with his pain. His grief has created a barrier of fear around him and
every moment is spent living behind it. No one can calm his mind or
heart; they have taken on a life of their own. Why has God abandoned
him? The Accuser speaks his lies...

"How is Adonai protecting you now?"[46] The Accuser continues...
"My complaint is bitter; His hand is heavy in spite of my groaning.
If only I knew where to find Him; if only I could go to His dwell-
ing! I would state my case before Him and fill my mouth with arguments... Would He oppose me with great power? No, He would not
press charges against me. There an upright man could present his case
before Him, and I would be delivered forever from my judge. But if I
go to the east, He is not there; if I go to the west, I do not find Him.

---

[45] Accuser is another term for Satan: Job 1:6.

[46] Reference to Job 1:10. Satan accuses God of always protecting Job from harm.

When He is at work in the north, I do not see Him; when He turns to the south, I catch no glimpse of Him."[47] The Accuser sends his chill... "Yes, in what wind is Adonai now? He is nowhere."

Why did God allow the Accuser to come to him? Why did God give the Accuser permission to enter his life? Why is God still allowing the Accuser to speak to him? Job has been faithful since the beginning. He and his forefathers lived to only serve Yahweh. They dedicated their whole lives in service to Him. Should this not then make him an exception? He has expectations of his relationship with Yahweh. He comes from Seth; he is a favored one, why is he now cursed?[48] His entire way of life and thought is now loss. His understanding of his El Shaddai is now muddled with confusion and disillusionment. No one can give him answers. There is no family left and no friends with wisdom.[49] Nothing is left... no peace, no quiet... just pain. All he has left is his turmoil and the deceit of the Accuser in his ear...

"Adonai could have stopped me, but He did not."

Job tries to recollect how it all began. First, it was all of his land and livelihood... and then... then the children. Job's children were too much to ask of him. God told Job He would never give him more than he can handle, but how far does He think Job's limits are?[50] Having his children dead is more than he can handle. The Accuser continues to steal...

"All you love is gone. Adonai took everything away, even your children..."

Then a new day came and with it, disease and curses on Job's body.[51] Unending suffering crippled him. The Accuser never ceases...

"Why were you born? What good is a life like this?" The Accuser continues to rob... "Let the day of my birth be erased... Why was I not

---

[47] Job 23:1-9
[48] Reference to Job 1:8—God said Job was blameless.
[49] Three of Job's friends try to counsel him, but fail.
[50] Reference to 1 Corinthians 10:13.
[51] Reference to Job 2:4-7.

born dead? Why did I not die as I came from the womb?... Had I died
at birth, I would now be at peace. I would be asleep and at rest... I cannot eat for sighing; my groans pour out like water. What I always feared
has happened to me... I have no peace, no quietness. I have no rest; only
trouble comes."[52] The Accuser influences...

"Listen to my thoughts... 'If my misery could be weighed and my
troubles be put on the scales, they would outweigh all the sands of the
sea... For the Almighty has struck me down with His arrows. Their
poison infects my spirit... Oh, that I might have my request, that God
would grant my desire. I wish He would crush me. I wish He would
reach out His hand and kill me... I don't have the strength to endure.
I have nothing to live for... Have I begged for anything of Yours for
myself? Have I asked You to rescue me from my enemies, or to save me
from ruthless people? Teach me, and I will keep quiet. Show me what I
have done wrong... Look at me!'"[53]

Job's tears can no longer make sound. He is nothing as he lies in
a pile of his own misery. God is not coming, only the Accuser. The
Accuser will not leave. The Accuser's lies separate...

"Morning will never come—you will live in this darkness for all of
your days. There is no sleep to rescue you." The Accuser pets Job's head...
"Lying in bed, I think, 'When will it be morning?' But the night drags
on, and I toss till dawn. My body is covered with maggots and scabs.
My skin breaks open, oozing with pus. My days... end without hope. O
God, remember that my life is but a breath, and I will never again feel
happiness... I must express my anguish. My bitter soul must complain...
I think, 'My bed will comfort me, and sleep will ease my misery,' but
then You shatter me with dreams and terrify me with visions. I would
rather be strangled—rather die than suffer like this. I hate my life and
don't want to go on living... Why make me Your target?"[54]

---

[52] Job 3 NLT
[53] Job 6:2-28 NLT
[54] Job 7:4-20 NLT

Job stopped asking long ago "why him"—he knows it does not matter. Job no longer has breath to ask for anything but death. His lungs are dry from this desert of pain. The Accuser takes...

"Fill your lungs with my words." The Accuser breathes out his lies to Job's mouth... "He will not let me catch my breath, but fills me instead with bitter sorrows.[55] I am disgusted with my life... My bitter soul must complain. I will say to God, 'Don't simply condemn me—tell me the charge You are bringing against me... Why do You reject me...[56] You formed me with Your hands; You made me, yet now You completely destroy me...'[57] What He destroys cannot be rebuilt. When He puts someone in prison, there is no escape.[58] I cry out, 'Help!' but no one answers me... God has blocked my way so I cannot move. He has plunged my path into darkness... He has demolished me on every side, and I am finished, He has destroyed my hope."[59]

The Accuser destroys... "Stay in this pain; I will lead you through it."

The last glimmer of life in Job is only his faith. Exhausted and tested as it is, it is still there. Why, he does not know. All he understands is his love for his Lord is still greater than his pain. Job has never understood the purpose of his grief or the point of his misery. What benefit his agony and torment is remains a mystery to Job. Whatever game the Deceiver is playing with him needs to end, because Job can no longer be a pawn. All he has left is this glimmer of faith, so Job finds strength to lift his broken body, and looks into the Accuser's eyes. Through quiet tears he utters his first words. All that has been before has only come from the Deceiver's mouth.

"Naked I came from my mother's womb; and naked I will depart. The Lord gave and the Lord has taken away; may the name of the Lord

---

[55] Job 9:18 NLT
[56] Job 10:1-3 NLT
[57] Job 10:8 NLT
[58] Job 12:14 NLT
[59] Job 19:7-10 NLT

be praised. Though He slay me, yet will I trust in Him.[60] I waste away like rotting wood, like a moth-eaten coat.[61] But as for me, I know that my Redeemer lives, and He will stand upon the earth at last. And after my body has decayed, yet in my body I will see God! I will see Him for myself. Yes, I will see Him with my own eyes. I am overwhelmed at the thought![62] I vow by the living God, who has taken away my rights, by the Almighty who has embittered my soul—As long as I live, while I have breath from God, my lips will speak no evil, and my tongue will speak no lies."[63]

Job collapses and prepares to die, too exhausted to do anything else. The serpent has squeezed Job so tightly that there is no breath left in him. The Devil is the author of this pain. The Accuser has finished Job.

A whirlwind comes upon the Accuser, and he hears the voice of his Lord.[64] The Accuser trembles for he knows he has gone too far. The Accuser has been the puppet master pulling Job's strings, using his hand to speak Job's words for too long. The Accuser knows the Father will make everything good again.

The Lord's fury is great, and His words create a tornado around the Devil. "Who is this that questions my wisdom with such ignorant words?"[65]

The Accuser tries to shout back; his rage is filling him. He has been controlling Job for too long, and does not want to give him back. But the Father shuts his mouth and crushes him down; He does not allow him to speak. Adonai summons the Accuser to his knees, and the Almighty questions his lies...

"Brace yourself because I have some questions for you, and you must answer them. Where were you when I laid the foundations of the

---

[60] Job 1:21 NLT
[61] Job 13:28 NLT
[62] Job 19:25-27 NLT
[63] Job 27:2-4 NLT
[64] Reference to Job 38:1.
[65] Job 38:2 NLT

earth?... Do you know how its dimensions were determined and who did the surveying? What supports its foundations, and who laid its cornerstone as the morning stars sang together and all the angels shouted for joy?"[66] The Father's holiness strangles all of the Devil's words of protest. The Almighty continues...

"Who defined the boundaries of the sea... Have you ever commanded the morning to appear or caused the dawn to rise in the east? Have you ever told the daylight to spread to the ends of the earth, to bring an end to night's wickedness?... Where does the light come from, and where does the darkness go? Can you take it to its home?... Can you hold back the movements of the stars? Can you ensure the proper sequence of the seasons or guide the constellations...? Do you know the laws of the universe and how God rules the earth?[67] Are you as strong as God, and can you thunder with a voice like His?"[68]

The Father of all creation grabs the Devil and chokes him...

"Who will confront me and remain safe? Everything under heaven is mine."[69]

The Father throws the Devil away, casting him out of Job's life forever. The Father sees how broken Job is, and His Spirit comes to breathe life into Job. Job is able to rise up. Then softly, the Father prays with Job.

"Is it better to know the answers or to know I am your Lord? Know I Am the God of this universe, and all of My ways are good and perfect. I Am the Great I Am; everything I create is used for My glory. You are My creation, and I will use your life for My glory. The Deceiver has been with you, but it has been allowed for My glorification. I will accomplish mighty things with your suffering."

Job begins crying, "I was searching for justice for my grief."

---

[66] Job 38:3-7 NLT
[67] Job 38:8-33 NLT
[68] Job 40:9 NLT
[69] Job 41:11 NLT

"Can any man question My justice? All justice is through Me and given only by Me. Only I can bring justice. Only I can bring blessings."

Job feels regret for allowing the Accuser to have his voice and words. He never meant to allow the Accuser into his heart and mind.

"Why me? 'I am nothing, how could I ever find the answers? I will put my hand over my mouth in silence. I have said too much already. I have nothing more to say.'"[70]

"My dear son, you are My favored one—My love for you knows no bounds. I have been with you through your suffering... I know your love for Me is true, and your faith is only based on that love. It is a faith that will be an example to the world for all time. It is a faith that is a testament to My plan and will see it achieved. Yes, I allowed a time of testing. I wanted to reveal your faith and refine it, so I could use it. The Deceiver tried to tempt you to cause you to sin and to fall from My glory, but My tests will make you stand. Your eyes are limited and they are trapped by time; but My eyes can see all, and your time of testing will provide a way for all. You learned to be patient and rest in your trust for Me. Through your suffering you learned to come to Me."

"'I know that you can do anything, and no one can stop you... Now I have seen you with my own eyes. I take back everything I said, and I sit in dust and ashes to show my repentance.'[71] I will never use my lack of understanding as an excuse for my lack of trust in You. I freely admit to You, my Lord, that I did not have enough faith to trust in You, so I trusted in the Accuser's lies more. I rested in them, and used his words as my cries out to You. Now my faith begins in my humility. Whether my restoration comes in this life or the next, I know You love me and are just. My restoration will come in eternity with you."

---

[70] Job 40:3–5 NLT
[71] Job 42:5–6 NLT

The Three come to Job and embrace him. It has pained Them to see the suffering Job has endured. The Father feels regret once more.[72] The Deceiver spoke a lie and the world fell. The Father knows His children will never understand why He allows the Deceiver to walk the earth. The Deceiver will create ballads of suffering and destruction from one generation to the next. The children will not know it is the Deceiver that is the author of the pain, and it is only the Father that can change the ballads for good. The Father takes Job's ballad and makes it good.[73] The Father knows that even through His children's confusion, His love will always hold true. His plan will restore everything.

---

[72] Reference to Genesis 6:6.
[73] Reference to Job 42:16-17.

LOVE'S ANALOGY

God tested Abraham. He said to him, "Abraham?" "Here I am," he replied. Then God said, "Take your son, your only son, whom you love—Isaac—and go to the region of Moriah. Sacrifice him there as a burnt offering on a mountain I will show you." Early the next morning Abraham got up and loaded his donkey. He took with him two of his servants and his son Isaac. When he had cut enough wood for the burnt offering, he set out for the place God had told him about. On the third day Abraham looked up and saw the place in the distance. He said to his servants, "Stay here with the donkey while I and the boy go over there. We will worship and then we will come back to you." Abraham took the wood for the burnt offering and placed it on his son Isaac, and he himself carried the fire and the knife. As the two of them went on together, Isaac spoke up and said to his father Abraham, "Father?" "Yes, my son?" Abraham replied. "The fire and wood are here," Isaac said, "but where is the lamb for the burnt offering?" Abraham answered, "God himself will provide the lamb for the burnt offering, my son." And the two of them went on together. When they reached the place God had told him about, Abraham built an altar there and arranged the wood on it. He bound his son Isaac and laid him on the altar, on top of the wood. Then he reached out his hand and took the knife to slay his son. But the angel of the Lord called out to him from heaven, "Abraham! Abraham!" "Here I am," he replied. "Do not lay a hand on the boy," he said. "Do not do anything to him. Now I know that you *fear God, because you have not withheld from me your son, your only son." Abraham looked up and there in a thicket he saw a ram caught by its horns. He went over and took the ram and sacrificed it as a burnt offering instead of his son. So Abraham called that place The Lord Will Provide. And to this day it is said, "On the mountain of the Lord it will be provided."*

Genesis 22:1-14

He who did not spare his own Son, but gave him up for us all—how will he not also, along with him, graciously give us all things?

Romans 8:32

By faith Abraham, when he was called, obeyed by going out to a place which he was to receive for an inheritance; and he went out, not knowing where he was going.

Hebrews 11:8

A blanket of darkness covers the sky, and sleep has just found his eyes when he hears a voice.

"Wake up."

Isaac does not need to look; he knows the voice.

"Yahweh."

"Yes."

Isaac sits up and is ready.

"How can I serve You?"

"I am going to send you on a journey tomorrow with your father. It will be a long journey, but My Spirit will walk with you the entire way. My Spirit has always been with you, preparing you for this day for years."

"I am Your servant, just tell me what You need of me and it will be done."

"I have known your servant's heart before I laid down the foundations of this world. And now I look at the man you have become—strong and faithful, the reasons why I chose you to fulfill My plan."[74]

"How can I be used in a plan of Yours? Why me? Who am I to be anything to You? It is my father who is Your friend—I am just his son."[75]

"You are My everything. You are the promised son whose line will bring salvation for all of My children. Yes, your father is one of My greatest friends; a man like no other, but you are the laugh that fills his spirit.[76] And you will carry My name to all of the world."

"Yahweh, I will give You my life. Tell me what I have to do."

"You have to carry the wood and trust in Me."

The Spirit comes upon Isaac. Isaac falls to his knees and begins to pray. He prays all night; sleep never touches his eyes again. He is not sure what to pray for, but he feels there is an urgency needed in his prayers. His body feels weak and human. He is angry at the limits of his human body; words are not enough. He wills his body to worship the Father, but it is not enough. He cannot tell the Father enough how much he loves Him. The tears, the praises, and the prayers are not enough. Isaac feels desperate; he needs more and more of the Father. Something in his soul tells him that tomorrow he will need to have more faith than ever. What is this torment in his soul, he cannot say, but he trusts the Father. He continues to pray all night.

Dawn is just approaching; a light haze is beginning to break the gray in the sky. The Father whispers to Abraham.

"It is time."

Abraham is already awake. He has never slept. This has been the longest night of his life. Abraham's only friend right now is confusion. He does not understand the request the Lord made of him yesterday. He has given his whole life to God in service and love, and now God

---

[74] Theologians estimate Isaac was in his late teens or early twenties at this point.

[75] The Bible states that Abraham was "a friend of God": James 4:4.

[76] Isaac means "he laughs."

has asked him to give up his son? He must have misunderstood, but he always comes back to Yahweh's words...

"Take your son, your only son Isaac, whom you love so much, and go to the land of Moriah. Sacrifice him there as a burnt offering..."[77]

Sacrifice? No, Yahweh could not have meant that! Abraham keeps telling himself that God will provide a way and an answer, but doubt keeps echoing in his mind. His soul begs...

"Please stop this now! Please, oh please, do not take him away from me. How can I live without him? This is too much to ask of a parent. I cannot give Isaac back to You; I'm not that strong. I need him here with me, not in heaven with You. Lord, this is not fair; I do not think I can be this kind of servant to You."

God hears his doubts. "You doubt me."

"I do not want to."

"You doubt if you can love Me more than Isaac."

Abraham becomes silent. His Friend has seen through to his heart. He has waited for so long for the promise of Isaac; how could God take him away now?[78] God promised the world would rest on Isaac's shoulders, why is He changing His covenant now? He feels shame for having that doubt, but it is there. Getting louder and louder with every breath he takes.

"Be My example."

"Lord, I do not know what that means."

"Get ready. Get the wood. Trust Me."

Abraham struggles to take a breath, but manages to stand. He makes his way outside and prepares for the journey. He gathers supplies and loads them onto his donkey. Then with a heavy heart he cuts the wood. Isaac does not wait to be instructed; he gathers the wood from his father and straps it to his back. Abraham has to blink away tears at the sight of Isaac carrying the wood. The instrument of his death will be

---

[77] Genesis 22:2
[78] Abraham was 100 years old when Isaac was born.

carried on his back for miles. Abraham does not understand, but the Spirit comes to Isaac and he is at peace. Abraham and Isaac set out for the long journey...

The Father and Son set out to accomplish the plan... The beloved Son that was so long waited for. So long needed, so long desperately prayed for, so long promised was finally here. Born from a miracle, the Son came with a plan on His shoulders. The plan to bring everlasting love into the world...

Isaac's feet never feel heavy, the Spirit is with him, and his heart is at complete peace. He looks to his father and can see stress in the lines of his face. This is his burden; a task that weighs heavily on the father's heart...

"Carry the wood" is all the Son can focus on. That is His job. The Father leads on, and the Son follows, obediently carrying the wood. The Son feels the Spirit. He is constantly whispering in His ear, "I will protect you. I will build my foundation on Your shoulders." He feels no fear, only trust in His Father's plan...

"Carry the wood on your back." Isaac just repeats that to himself as he walks up the mountain. With every step, he utters, "Carry the wood..."

The Son looks to the Father as He marches on. He does not feel resentment or anger; He understands the need for the plan. Death entered against God's perfect design, causing us to be separated. He had to create a plan to resolve it; a sacrifice has to be exchanged...

"Carry the wood," Isaac repeats to himself.

The Spirit comes and lifts the load for Isaac. Miles have passed, but his feet still do not feel heavy. He trusts in God, but Abraham's heart is in pure torment. His feet are cracked and bleeding from the stress of the journey. As they walk, Abraham's heart is screaming.

"Please stop this now! Please, oh please, I cannot watch him being taken away from me."

But Abraham marches forward.

"How can I live without him, even for just a moment?"

Abraham marches forward.

"I cannot allow the pain. I cannot allow all the darkness to fall on his shoulders."

The Father knows the darkness has to fall on the Son. The plan was for His children to be with Him always. The plan was for nothing to ever separate them. The plan was a love story between Him and the children. Then darkness entered and diseased His plan, and now the price to fix it is a sacrifice. No one will ever know the pain this sacrifice causes the Father...

Abraham marches on with tears in his eyes. For three days the father and son march on toward the mountain...

... Marching toward a tomb of despair. For three days the promised Son will be in a tomb of despair before the salvation comes...[79]

Then Abraham and Isaac come to the bottom of the mountain; their journey is not done. The Father looks down on Abraham and his son. Abraham looks up to the Father with tears choking his eyes. Abraham says a prayer, giving God his last ounce of trust. With only faith to give him confidence, Abraham tells the servants to stay behind and assures them that *both* he and the boy will return shortly.[80] Abraham's heart cries out to the Father, "I trust you," as he and Isaac hike up the mountain.

That is the moment. That is the moment God is looking for. He always knew His great friend loved Him more than any earthly blessing He had given him, but it was that moment when Abraham became the example.

Isaac recognizes the mountain, realizes they have not brought a sacrifice, and questions his father.

"Father, we have the wood and the fire, but where is the lamb for the sacrifice?"[81]

The Spirit hears Isaac's troubled heart and whispers into his ear, "Trust in Me."

---

[79] It took Abraham and Isaac three days to march to the mountain, and Jesus spent three days in the tomb after the crucifixion.

[80] Reference to Genesis 22:5.

[81] Genesis 22:7 TLB

"God will provide a lamb, my son,"[82] the words cracking out of Abraham's mouth.

Abraham prepares the altar. He looks to the ropes and his eyes fill with tears. How can he do this? Why cannot it be him instead? He quietly pleads with the Lord, "Please let the ropes be for me."

Isaac looks at the altar and his father, and he understands. The Spirit catches the panic in his breath and whispers, "My ways are perfect, this place is perfect, and My Son is perfect. Be still, and allow Me to enter your heart so I can have My work accomplished."

Isaac looks to the altar again and sees all of its beautiful glory, and he places his hand on Abraham's shoulder tenderly.

"Father, trust in your Friend. Put the ropes on me."

Abraham looks up with tears blurring his vision, and blindly he begins to tie ropes on his child. He then takes his son and lays him upon the altar. Isaac tells him that his knife is strapped to his leg. Abraham looks at the knife for a long moment—he cannot will his hand to even touch it.

"Father, take my knife. Trust your Friend."

Abraham takes the knife, and then a great thunder from heaven comes upon them.

"Abraham! Abraham!"[83]

Abraham cannot breathe; he has to grab onto the altar to hold his weak body from falling from his shock and hope.

He cries out desperately, "Yes! Yes, I'm listening..."

"Lay down the knife. Do not hurt the boy in any way, for now I know that you truly fear God. You have not withheld even your beloved son from me."[84]

Abraham can no longer maintain the weight of his body and falls to the ground. The Spirit comes and lifts him to his feet, fills his lungs

---

[82] Genesis 22:8 TLB
[83] Genesis 22:11 TLB
[84] Genesis 22:12 TLB

with breath, and God sends the real sacrifice. The substitute is provided, and Abraham races to untie the ropes and embrace his son. He knows this was not a test; this was a refining. Abraham needed to know what God already knew of him—that he was strong enough to walk up that mountain. Abraham loved his Father and was ready to be the example the Lord needed him to be. He was strong enough to show the world God's plan. Then God speaks one more time to both of them.

"You are My faithful servants, but there is only one Son that can be My sacrifice. And only one Father who can do the task."

Abraham and Isaac walk back down the mountain to join the servants.

LOVE'S BLESSING

So Jacob was left alone, and a man wrestled with him till daybreak. When the man saw that he could not overpower him, he touched the socket of Jacob's hip so that his hip was wrenched as he wrestled with the man. Then the man said, "Let me go, for it is daybreak." But Jacob replied, "I will not let you go unless you bless me." The man asked him, "What is your name?" "Jacob," he answered. Then the man said, "Your name will no longer be Jacob, but Israel, because you have struggled with God and man and have overcome." ... So Jacob called the place Peniel, saying, "It is because I saw God face to face, and yet my life was spared."

Genesis 32:24-28, 30

For now, we see only a reflection as in a mirror; then we shall see face to face. Now I know in part; then I shall know fully, even as I am fully known.

1 Corinthians 13:12

Get rid of all bitterness, rage and anger, brawling and slander, along with every form of malice. Be kind and compassionate to one another, forgiving each other, just as in Christ God forgave you.

Ephesians 4:31-32

.... that I may gain Christ and be found in him, not having a righteousness of my own that comes from the law, but that which is through faith in Christ... Not that I have already obtained all this, or have already arrived at my goal, but I press on to take hold of that for which Christ Jesus took hold of me. Brothers and sisters, I do not consider myself yet to have taken hold of it. But one thing I do: Forgetting what is behind and straining toward what is ahead, I press on toward the goal to win the prize for which God has called me heavenward in Christ Jesus.

Philippians 3:8-9, 12-14

In the darkness, Jacob can barely make out the Man's form. He understands that the Man has been chasing after him for a long time—his whole life. Jacob has felt the Man's presence from the first moment he can remember. Jacob realizes he can no longer run away; it is time to face the Man.

Years of deceit, tricks, and falsehoods have broken Jacob. He has been a disappointment to his father and grandfather. He could always feel God calling him for more, but now what does he have to give? What has he made out of his life? He is not the legacy. He is not the chosen one to carry on the plan. He stole the birthright from the one who rightfully deserved it.[85] Shame brought him to this lowly state.

He thinks of that day; the day he took everything away from his brother. He understood his brother's tendencies to be impulsive and not to think of the consequences. He took advantage of his weakened physical and emotional state, like a vulture attacking an injured animal. Then that was not enough; he had to continue on with his deceit and steal his brother's blessing too. His mother told him he was to be great, that the Lord declared it, but neither she nor he could wait on the Lord's plan. Had God forgotten His promise to them? They were unsure, and convinced themselves they needed to make the Lord's promise happen

---

[85] Jacob tricked his older brother Esau to give over his birthright in Genesis 27.

for themselves. Selfishness is always the way the Deceiver attacks. Now Jacob wonders what his life would have been if he had waited on the Lord. Would his path be glorious instead of one of hiding in the shadows? This path has led him to deceit, and deceit followed him throughout his journey of escape. He has been running away for so long and he longs for his home once more. But he can never go back. All is lost to him—his mother, his father, his brother, and his character. Now Jacob's actions have taken him tumbling down a mountain instead of running victoriously up it. For the first time he questions what his actions have done to his brother. He was too selfish before to ask that, but now it is all he can think of. Guilt eats away at his soul like cancer.

Years before, there was that night... the night with his dream... that stairway...[86] God came to him in all of His glory promising the world to Jacob. God called him, but he is still unsure. Was the dream real? Over the years he questioned that more than anything. Why would God still want him after everything he has done? It must have been a mistake, and God just needs to move on to someone else. He is not his grandfather, the great friend of the Almighty.[87] He is not his father, the chosen son.[88] Jacob has questioned "why me" for years, all the while knowing he is not good enough for God's plan.

But now the Man is here. Jacob does not understand; he is on his way to make peace with his brother. Is that not what God wanted from him? Jacob wants to surrender, knowing he must pay for all of his sins, but something is burning inside of him. He needs to fight. All he feels is anger. Anger at himself for being such a disappointment, and he has to punch the anger out of himself. He needs to put the anger on someone else; he cannot bear to feel it any longer.

The Man is closer now, and His image becomes clear. The Man is here to wrestle the demons out of Jacob. All night long they fight

---

[86] Reference to Genesis 28:10-22.
[87] Reference to Abraham.
[88] Reference to Isaac.

with each other. Jacob's need to survive turns into his need to be accepted. He does not know if he needs acceptance from God or from himself. Is Jacob wrestling the Man or his inner self? He no longer knows; he just feels his body continuing. Exhaustion never comes, just the fight.

The Man wants to enter into Jacob's heart, but he continues to fight Him. The Man asks the Father how much longer it will take, and the Father says, "Just a little longer. He is not ready yet." So the Man wrestles longer.

Jacob screams out in pain. Not from physical pain, but the pain he has carried in his heart all of these years.

"Bless me!"

The Man remains silent.

"Bless me!"

The Man remains silent. He knows that Jacob does not know yet what he is asking for. Jacob does not understand that God's blessing means he has to turn over his control. Jacob can no longer be self-reliant, but must give his life entirely to the Lord. The Lord has been waiting for so long for this moment. He has called Jacob since the beginning. The Three knew even at creation that Jacob had to be the one to carry on the plan. But Jacob has been running away for so long, denying his need for the Lord.

"Bless me!"

The Man begins to tire of this constant battle. Jacob's heart is not surrendering.

"Tell me... why me?"

The Man knows He needs to humble Jacob, so He touches Jacob's hip, and causes it to fall out of joint.[89]

Then the Man says, "Let me go, for it is dawn."[90]

---

[89] Reference to Genesis 32:25.
[90] Genesis 32:26 NLT

"I will not let you go unless you bless me. Please, I beg of You. I am ready."[91]

"What is your name?" the Man asks.[92]

"Jacob."

The Man becomes frustrated. Jacob has to surrender his heart fully. With only a lift of the Man's finger, Jacob feels the pain of his hip rush down his leg.

"What is your name?" the Man asks again.

"Whatever you call me is who I am."

He submitted; it is now time. The plan can move forward.

"Your name will no longer be Jacob," the Man tells him, "It is now Israel, because you have struggled with both God and men and have won. You were once an ambitious deceiver, and now you are Israel... the one who struggles with God and overcomes. I told you before that 'I will be with you, and I will protect you wherever you go... I will be with you constantly until I have finished giving you everything I have promised.'"[93]

"What is your name?" Jacob asks of the Man.[94]

"Why do you ask?" the Man questions.[95]

The Man knows that question comes from Jacob's need to control. The sinful desire is still lurking within his heart. God has willingly revealed Himself to Jacob over and over again, assuring Jacob that He will keep His covenant to him. Jacob's remaining pride and control are hindering him from seeing what God has just done for him tonight... He has given Jacob a new name. Jacob's new name is the revelation of God's name forever. The Man searches Jacob's soul. He looks and looks, but He only sees Jacob. He has to make Jacob understand this; the Man calls the Spirit to come.

---

[91] Genesis 32:26 NLT

[92] Genesis 32:27 NLT

[93] Genesis 32:28, Israel means "God struggles" or "one who struggles with God."

[94] Genesis 32:29 NLT

[95] Genesis 32:29 NLT

The Spirit comes, enters Jacob, and opens his eyes. Jacob gasps for breath, but cannot find it. Jacob knows the One he has wrestled all night... he recognizes the Son.[96] The Spirit blows a new breath and Jacob feels a love inside of himself that is new. God's love. The guilt is no more. He is God's chosen child. After all the years of deceit, lies, and sin, God still chose him. God wanted Jacob so much He wrestled him for hours just to reach him. God loved Jacob so much that He gave him a new name. Jacob understands the narrative of his life has changed. Jacob is no longer the liar and cheat; he is the one who rises above his struggles. Jacob will fulfill God's ultimate plan. No matter how many hardships and how much persecution may come, Israel will prevail and overcome.[97] A name change is not what he will be called, but who he will become. That is the blessing Jacob seeks.

Then suddenly the Son stops seeing Jacob, but sees Israel, and finally blesses him.[98] The birthright is now complete. The Son leaves and the sun is rising. Jacob is limping from the pain of his hip, but he leaves Peniel.[99]

---

[96] Many scholars believe Jacob was wrestling Jesus all night.

[97] The country of Israel, throughout history, will struggle.

[98] Reference to Genesis 32:29.

[99] Jacob named the place Peniel, which means "face of God.".

LOVE'S ACCEPTANCE

Now Laban had two daughters; the name of the older was Leah, and the name of the younger was Rachel. Leah had weak eyes, but Rachel had a lovely figure and was beautiful. Jacob was in love with Rachel and said, "I'll work for you seven years in return for your younger daughter Rachel." Laban said, "It's better that I give her to you than to some other man. Stay here with me." So Jacob served seven years to get Rachel, but they seemed like only a few days to him because of his love for her. Then Jacob said to Laban, "Give me my wife. My time is completed, and I want to make love to her." So Laban brought together all the people of the place and gave a feast. But when evening came, he took his daughter Leah and brought her to Jacob, and Jacob made love to her... When morning came, there was Leah! So Jacob said to Laban, "What is this you have done to me? I served you for Rachel, didn't I? Why have you deceived me?" Laban replied, "It is not our custom here to give the younger daughter in marriage before the older one. Finish this daughter's bridal week; then we will give you the younger one also, in return for another seven years of work." And Jacob did so. He finished the week with Leah, and then Laban gave him his daughter Rachel to be his wife... Jacob made love to Rachel also, and his love for Rachel was greater than his love for Leah... When the Lord saw that Leah was not loved, he enabled her to conceive, but Rachel remained childless. Leah became pregnant and gave birth to a son.

Genesis 29:1-23, 25-28, 30-32

Blessed are the poor in spirit, for theirs is the kingdom of heaven.

Matthew 5:3

*May you experience the love of Christ, though it is too great to understand
fully. Then you will be made complete with all the fullness of life and power
that comes from God.*

Ephesians 3:19 NLT

*Your beauty should not come from outward adornment... Rather, it should be
that of your inner self, the unfading beauty of a gentle and quiet spirit, which
is of great worth in God's sight.*

1 Peter 3:3-4

Leah sits quietly in the corner. Always in the corner and always quiet. He never cares what she has to say anyway. She has been with him for over seven years, and he still never looks at her. She knows she is not pretty and doesn't have interesting thoughts, but in her heart, she knows she has something to give. Why can Jacob not see it? Why can Jacob not love her?

At first, Leah did not resent Jacob; she knew he did not love her. She knew he loved Rachel. Rachel loved Jacob too. At first, Leah felt like an intruder on their love. She did feel hurt that yet another man looked at Rachel and not her, but she saw the truth in his eyes and was content to let them love each other. It was not her idea to betray their trust. She was thrust into the center of their love story unwillingly. It only made her feel more unloved, and it crushed her heart to have a man look so displeased to wake up next to her. Now, seven years later, she is here. Seven years of waking up to disappointment on Jacob's face. Now the displeasure fuels an anger in her that is deep. Why does she not deserve love too? Why does she not deserve a man to look at her longingly? Why does she not deserve Jacob's heart? She has been humiliated over and over again by a love she cannot have. For the past seven years she has just existed in this twisted love story, feeling nothing but unwanted, undesired, and unloved. She no longer misses the sisterhood she once had with Rachel; all she can think of is her pain. Her excruciating anguish of not being loved.

Her hours are spent on her knees begging God to take her pain away. Leah is consumed in her prayers, pleading with God to bring her love. The Lord sees her plight, and He blesses her with a son.

"I shall name him Reuben, for Adonai has seen my misery. Surely my husband will love me now."[100]

Jacob's love does not come. It never does. So Leah's prayers continue, and the Lord blesses her again. She gives birth to another son.

"Because Adonai heard that I am not loved, He gave me this one too. So I will name him Simeon."[101]

Still no peace comes. She does not understand why God does not make Jacob love her. How can she ever be content without his love? Again, God allows Leah to conceive and give birth to another son.

"Now at last, my husband will become attached to me, because I have borne him three sons. So I will name him Levi."[102]

Jacob still does not love her. She drops to her knees once more.

"Why me, Adonai?"

She quietly repeats that question in her mind over and over. She has asked it for seven years. Why is she the one who is always omitted, overlooked, and unloved?

"Do You not understand how broken I am? Do You not understand I cannot even breathe anymore because of the heartache! Why do You not help me?"

She does not understand why God does not grant this prayer. Is it not right for a man to love his wife? Is it not God's plan? Why has the

---

[100] Reference to Genesis 29:32. Adonai is a name for God meaning "my master." Reuben means "look, a son" in Hebrew.
[101] Reference to Genesis 29:33. Simeon means "one who hears" in Hebrew.
[102] Reference to Genesis 9:34. Levi means "feeling affection for" in Hebrew.

Father left her in this state of solitude and heartache? Was it not God's will for her to be a wife? For years, she has devoted her life to serving Jacob and fulfilling his every need. Leah has made Jacob the center of her world, and the Lord has never moved Jacob's heart. She does not understand, and feels nothing but defeat. She cries out to the Lord...

"Adonai, what is your plan? Am I so unworthy to have love? Why are You not providing more for my life? Why do You not make my husband love me? I cannot live like this any longer, and You do not do anything to help me. Adonai, why? Please, I beg You, come and help me. I have given my everything to Jacob, why do You give me nothing now?"

Leah is exhausted and defeated. She has no more left to give to Jacob. God looks down upon her. He sees her broken heart, but knows it is broken for the wrong reason. For years, her need for acceptance has blinded her from her heart's real desire: Him. The Father has been patient for Leah to realize she needs Him more than she needs Jacob.

The Spirit whispers to Leah's heart.

"Yes, you have given everything to Jacob, but I ask you to give everything to Me. Trust in Me; I want to include you in My plan."

Leah has never felt included in anything before. The Deceiver tells her again that it is a trick, and she is not good enough to be included. Leah crawls back into her pit, but keeps hearing the Spirit whisper to her.

The Father will give her one more chance to see the truth. The Lord blesses her one more time. The Father gives her one more son. Leah looks down at her son. The baby is not like the others before him. Is it the baby or her? Is it her heart that has changed? She does not see Jacob in him, nor does she feel sorrow any longer. She feels exhaustion. She is too tired to want Jacob any longer. She wants acceptance; she wants peace. Leah wants to feel love. Leah wants to feel an everlasting, true love, that will fill her emptiness. She looks down to her son and says, "This time I will praise the Lord. I will call him Judah."[103]

---

[103] Reference to Genesis 9:35: Judah means "praise" in Hebrew.

The Spirit comes and fills her with His breath. Leah feels love and peace in her heart for the first time.

"Now I will praise the Lord!"[104]

God is pleased. She finally turns away from her grief to praise God first. Her pain is not resolved; she and the Father both know it, but she decides to praise God despite the pain. She does not want Jacob any longer—she wants God. Leah's dependence on Jacob for love has now turned toward the Father. She depends only on Him. The Father's plan can move forward; the Son can come. The Father will bless her, and love her more than she could ever desire. Leah has pleased Him, and He will honor her by making His scepter pass to the one whose name means praise.[105]

---

[104] Genesis 9:35

[105] Jesus comes from the line of David, who comes from the line of Judah.

LOVE'S SALVATION

Tell the whole community of Israel that on the tenth day of this month each man is to take a lamb... The animals you choose must be year-old males without defect... Take care of them until the fourteenth day of the month, when all the members of the community of Israel must slaughter them at twilight. Then they are to take some of the blood and put it on the sides and tops of the doorframes of the houses where they eat the lambs... it is the LORD's Passover. On that same night the Destroyer will pass through Egypt and strike down every firstborn of both people and animals, and I will bring judgment on all the gods of Egypt. I am the LORD. The blood will be a sign for you on the houses where you are, and when I see the blood, I will pass over you. No destructive plague will touch you when I strike Egypt... Go at once and select the animals for your families and slaughter the Passover lamb. Take a bunch of hyssop, dip it into the blood in the basin and put some of the blood on the top and on both sides of the doorframe... When the LORD goes through the land to strike down the Egyptians, he will see the blood on the top and sides of the doorframe and will pass over that doorway, and he will not permit the destroyer to enter your houses and strike you down.

Exodus 12:3, 5-7, 12-13, 21-23

The next day John saw Jesus coming toward him and said, "Look! There is the Lamb of God who takes away the sin of the world!"

John 1:29

Christ, our Passover Lamb, has been sacrificed for us.

1 Corinthians 5:7

For you know that God paid a ransom to save you from the empty life you inherited from your ancestors. And it was not paid with mere gold or silver, which lose their value. It was the precious blood of Christ, the sinless, spotless Lamb of God.

1 Peter 1:18-19

They will make war on the Lamb, and the Lamb will triumph over them, for he is Lord of lords and King of kings, and those with him are called and chosen and faithful followers.

Revelation 17:14

It is dawn on the tenth day and a sacrifice has to be chosen. Yahweh has commanded the sacrifice to be without defect. The Believer has been waiting for this time for so long; he was beginning to question if it would happen in his lifetime. The greatness of it weighs heavily on his shoulders; he will witness God's promised salvation. The Believer wanders through the flock, looking for the perfect lamb to sacrifice—it is the tenth day and he has to choose today. He looks toward the sky and calls out,

"Yahweh, provide the perfect sacrifice."

With his heart full of faith, he looks up and sees the sacrifice coming toward him. He has no doubts—the Spirit tells him this is the one, this is Yahweh's perfect lamb. The lamb is not what he has pictured in his mind all of these years. The Believer thought the lamb would be the biggest and grandest of them all, but this one is humble and small. The lamb comes gently toward him, but with confidence. The lamb seems to understand what his calling is and is at peace with it.[106]

For four days the Believer loves and nurtures his newfound lamb, but others in the family are in disbelief and inspect the lamb thoroughly. They cannot believe the lamb is without defect in any way. They put the lamb on trial in hope of finding a blemish in his white coat. Some succumb and relent, trusting that this lamb is the one to sacrifice, but others refuse to allow this one to be their salvation and they walk away. The Believer, too, once saw the lamb with doubt in his heart, but he sees the lamb differently now. What he once took for granted, he now finds so beautiful. When confusion clouds his mind, the lamb comes with his gentle nuzzle and brings truth. When fear enters his heart, the lamb comes and lies with him, and brings peace. When the pain of yesterday is too much for him to endure today, the lamb comes and offers his back to carry his burdens. And now, when the Believer's sin is too much for him to reconcile, the lamb comes and offers his blood for the Believer's salvation. The Believer understands the lamb now, and it breaks his heart to know that soon this beauty will have to end. It will end to save him. The beauty of the pure white soul will be tainted with dark red blood. The lamb's blood.

Twilight of the fourteenth day has come.[107] It is time to slay the lamb. It will be a slaughter and nothing short of it. Everything that has come before will not compare to the pain that will be felt tonight. The lamb has to be crucified for the salvation of all.

The Believer meets his lamb outside, and holds the lamb for the last time. He feels the lamb's breath on his hands, calm and steady. He knows it is time. A crowd has formed to watch. Some believe the sacrifice is done in vain, and will amount to nothing, but others believe in the sacrifice and are moved to tears.

---

[106] Reference to Exodus 12:5—the lamb must be a male without defect.

[107] On the tenth day of the month, the family chose the sacrifice, and on the evening of the fourteenth day, the sacrifice was slaughtered: Genesis 12.

First, he ties the lamb up. He then shaves off all of the lamb's hair. The lamb is stripped down to the skin. The Believer's knife has cut and torn the lamb's skin, but the lamb does not cry out. He now hooks the lamb onto an old wooden post and stretches the lamb's limbs across so it cannot move. It is time to get the blood. The Believer pierces the lamb and drains his lifeblood out. All is quiet, and the blood comes out steady and warm. Once the flow ceases, the Believer carefully takes down his savior. He is cautious not to disturb the lamb's body any further; not one bone will be broken. He sees his salvation in the lifeless body before him. The Believer wants to grieve, but he knows the job is not finished. He needs the covering of the blood.

It is time to purify the house. Hyssop is taken.[108] Against the hard, splintered wood he uses the hyssop to paint the blood. Up, down, and over. Crossing it over and over again. The once beautiful purple blossoms are stained with red.[109] He is surprised by how much blood there is—how much blood it takes to save him. The blood seals his soul from the Destroyer who is coming.[110]

The lamb is dead, the blood has been shed, and the house is marked... darkness falls. The earth shakes and trembles with fear; the Destroyer is on the move. The Believer holds his family in the quiet, only breathing the Spirit in; he knows no fear. The other children cry out with questions of why this is happening and what is next? But the Believer remains in his peace and praises the Father; his faith and trust are bigger than his questions. He knows his lamb will protect him. Yahweh promised this salvation from the beginning; it has always been a part of His plan.[111] The lamb's blood is Yahweh's plan. The blood creates a covering that is an impenetrable barrier to the Destroyer. The Believer knows that Yahweh Himself has laid His own body over his home to protect him. By the blood on the door, Yahweh is marking His people and giving them an exodus from the darkness forever.

---

[108] Hyssop plant was used in purifying rites by the ancient Hebrews.

[109] Hyssop has purple blossoms.

[110] Destroyer refers to the angel God sent to kill the firstborn.

[111] God instructed Adam and Eve to sacrifice a lamb to Him.

LOVE'S COMMUNION

God also said to Moses, "I am the Lord. I appeared to Abraham, to Isaac and to Jacob as God Almighty, but by my name the Lord I did not make myself fully known to them."

Exodus 6:2-3

He said, "Listen to my words: 'When there is a prophet among you, I, the Lord reveal myself to them in visions, I speak to them in dreams. But this is not true of my servant Moses; he is faithful in all my house. With him I speak face to face, clearly and not in riddles; he sees the form of the Lord. Why then were you not afraid to speak against my servant Moses?'"

Numbers 12:6-8

Then Moses climbed Mount Nebo from the plains of Moab to the top of Pisgah, across from Jericho. There the Lord showed him the whole land—from Gilead to Dan, all of Naphtali, the territory of Ephraim and Manasseh, all the land of Judah as far as the Mediterranean Sea, the Negev and the whole region from the Valley of Jericho, the City of Palms, as far as Zoar. Then the Lord said to him, 'This is the land I promised on oath to Abraham, Isaac, and Jacob when I said, 'I will give it to your descendants.' I have let you see it with your eyes, but you will not cross over into it." And Moses the servant of the Lord died there in Moab, as the Lord had said.

Deuteronomy 34:1-5

He was faithful to the one who appointed him,
just as Moses was faithful in all God's house.

Hebrews 3:2

The time has come. They walk up the mountain together. They are always together, even when others cannot see it. Moses never understood why, but he stopped asking long ago. For 120 years, Moses has been in the Lord's hands. There were times when those hands felt more merciful than others, but those hands never let go of him. Now it is time for it all to stop. This long journey is over, and Moses is ready.

After 120 years of close communion with each other, Moses knows this will be the last time the friends will fellowship together like this. The hike up the mountain is full of twists, steep steps, and dangerous cliffs, but the Father's hands help Moses reach the top. Moses is surprised he is not out of breath, but feels strong, almost like the man he was long ago.[112]

They sit together like they have done so many times before, but this time, quiet is all that is needed. Words are not essential anymore, there is too much love and trust for simple words to fill the silence. Never before or since has God ever favored anyone like Moses.[113]

Their relationship started before Moses could accept it. At the time of his birth, Moses was already a beautiful sight in God's eyes.[114] At three months of age, the Lord commissioned Moses's life by placing him in a little ta-va.[115] Like Noah's ark before him, Moses's ta-va was an ark of deliverance for all of God's children. The Lord looked down onto that basket and saw His friend; He saw His son.[116]

---

[112] Reference to Deuteronomy 34:7. At the time of his death the Bible states he was in good health.

[113] Reference to Deuteronomy 34:10.

[114] Reference to Acts 7:20.

[115] Exodus 2:2 and Acts 7:20 state that Moses was three months old when he was placed in the basket. Ta-va, the Hebrew word meaning "ark," was used in the Bible to describe the basket.

[116] Reference to Exodus 33:11.

A son growing up as an impostor prince, never knowing his place in the world. A son never understanding who he is. A son not understanding his worth. A son not understanding who his Father is. Moses is the one to bring change. Moses is the one to lead millions. Moses is the one whom the Father loves.

For years, God molded and cultivated Moses for His plan. Their relationship is not Master and servant, but Father and son. Full of tension, grief, arguments, tears, faith, and love. Love that tested, encouraged, and sustained Moses. A love that conquered and defined a nation. Together, God and Moses exodus out of the darkness.

So many times over the years Moses asked the Father, "Why me? Why did you send me?"[117]

God always responded with one answer. "Because you are meek."[118]

Again Moses would question, "Father, why did you send me?"

"Because you are meek."

There were times when that answer enraged Moses and he rebelled.[119] Then God would say...

"Moses, you are meek, more than all people who are on the face of the earth.[120] Son, you still do not understand. Meekness is 'enduring injury with patience and without resentment.'[121] The person who is meek is someone who is not occupied with self at all. It is a person who completely releases all that they are to serve another. Strength can only come from the meek. Love can only come from the meek. Blessed are the meek, for they shall inherit the earth."[122]

Eventually that answer gave Moses the strength he needed to continue on. He had to continue on... step after step, mile after mile, day after day, week after week, year after year... God asked him to continue on.

---

[117] Exodus 5:22 NLT
[118] Reference to Numbers 12:3.
[119] Reference to Numbers 20:1–13
[120] Reference to Numbers 12:3 KJV.
[121] Meek definition from Webster's Dictionary
[122] Matthew 5:5 KJV.

The Father gave him clouds by day and fire by night, guiding him through the plan.[123] So many had come before Moses who did not understand what incredible love existed in that guidance. Moses understood what extraordinary glory was in the clouds and fire. Moses was His chosen son.

Moses was instructed in all wisdom; he was mighty in his words and deeds.[124] Every time he became discouraged, the Father came to him and reminded Moses of the plan.

"I will give My law through you, Moses; and My grace and truth will come through the Son."[125]

That was all Moses ever needed to know to continue on. He knew his life was not his own, and he was commissioned for more. He was commissioned for the plan. Now his commission is over, and he is at the top of the mountain with his Father, the Son, and the Spirit.

The Father turns to Moses and instructs one last time.

"I want you to write one last song."[126]

He tells Moses the words one more time. Moses has been writing for so long—amazing stories of God's love and victory. God revealed the characters to Moses so well that he understood every moment, as though he had lived the stories himself. Moses was not the author, but an ordained participant. Yahweh put Adam's heart into Moses's heart, and he felt the struggle of temptation and the shame of wanting more. Yahweh put Noah's trepidation into Moses's soul, and he felt the battle of fighting the world alone. Yahweh put Abraham's faith into Moses's mind, and he felt the relief of trusting. Moses saw their stories and knew them. Yahweh put His hand over Moses's, and one last time together, they wrote His last song.

"Listen, O heavens, and I will speak! Hear, O earth, the words that I say! Let my teaching fall on you like rain; let my speech settle like

---

[123] Reference to the time the Israelites spent in the wilderness.
[124] Reference to Acts 7:22.
[125] Reference to John 1:17.
[126] Reference to Deuteronomy 32 and 33.

dew. Let my words fall like rain on tender grass, like gentle showers on young plants. I will proclaim the name of the Lord; how glorious is our God! He is the Rock; His deeds are perfect. Everything He does is just and fair. He is a faithful God who does no wrong; but they have acted corruptly toward Him; when they act so perversely, are they really His children? They are a deceitful and twisted generation. Is this the way you repay the Lord, you foolish and senseless people? Isn't He your Father who created you? Has He not made you and established you? How just and upright He is!"[127]

"But still... God loves you and His children will be defined. Indeed, You love the people; all Your holy ones are in Your hands. They follow in Your steps and accept Your instruction... There is no one like the God of Israel. He rides across the skies in majestic splendor. The eternal God is your refuge, and His everlasting arms are under you. He thrusts out the enemy before you; it is He who cries, 'Destroy them!'... How blessed you are, O Israel! Who else is like you, a people saved by the Lord? He is your protecting shield and your triumphant sword! Your enemies will bow low before you, and you will trample on their backs."[128]

The Spirit tells Moses to write everything His children will ever need to understand the plan. As Moses finishes the song, he feels the passionate euphoria turn into the melancholy remnants of a service concluding. His authorship time is over. Yahweh put His hand on his shoulder, the Spirit filled his lungs with His breath, and the Son sat next to him. He knows the Three. Moses knows them by name. A name he used over and over again in his writing, but a name that was never known to anyone like Moses knew it.[129] For so long, he did not understand the answer to the question "why me," but now he does. He laughs now at the thought of how complicated he once made it.

---

[127] Deuteronomy 32:1-6 NLT
[128] Deuteronomy 33:3-4, 26-29 NLT
[129] Reference to Exodus 6:2-3. The Bible states that God told Moses His name.

The Three know he is the only one who understands the answer, and that is why Moses knew Their names.

Moses had to be that baby floating down the river, the prince among the enemy, the one who faced the plagues, and the one who led the millions. All of that was to prepare Moses to know the Three and to see the Father's face. He knew the Lord face to face.[130] He never wanted things from Yahweh; he just wanted to see Yahweh's face. That is why he was chosen.

Now at the top of this mountain, Moses understands and no more questions are needed. They sit together there, remembering. There were times of doubt, times of pain, times of struggle, times of sin, but mostly there were times of trust, times of faith, times of salvation, and times of love. Moses recognizes his highs and lows along this journey, and all of the times he doubted or chose another way. He feels no vexation of the consequences of his choices. Moses understands now that it was never the Father's plan for him to enter the Promised Land. Moses's job is complete, and now it is time for the next child.[131] Yahweh wants Moses home with Him, and what land could be better than heaven?

Moses was entrusted with God's plan for so long. He was not delivering Israel, but preparing a way for the Son.

"Father."

"Yes?"

"The natural came first... You created Adam as a living being from the dust of the earth. An earthly man in need of rescue. You have entrusted me to be the rescuer of Adam's sons and show them Your plan."[132]

Moses looks to the Son.

"But I know my work is a parallel for You. You are the life-giving Adam. You are of heaven, to bring all of heaven to them. You are not

---

[130] Reference to Deuteronomy 34:10.

[131] Reference to Joshua.

[132] Reference to 1 Corinthians 15:45-49.

dust that can blow away or earth that ends once buried, but the spiritual that will last for eternity.[133] Noah saved one, I saved a generation, and You will save all. My job is done."

God sees the meekness in his heart, and knows Moses understands His plan better than anyone else.

"It is time to show you My Promised Land. This is the land I promised on oath to Abraham, Isaac, and Jacob, and I told them I would give it to their descendants."[134]

The Spirit opens Moses's eyes to see. God shows Moses across the entire land. Moses is able to see every tree, every hill, every animal, and every part of His beautiful creation. Moses looks to the Three with tears in his eyes and a smile on his lips.

"My Lord, for forty years this land has directed all of my footsteps... no, even long before that. Here I am seeing it all for the first time, and it is nothing. I once thought I would find Your glory here, but it is not here. Not after seeing Your face. Your children will chase the land, and they will not understand that it is nothing. I can see that for years to come, they will believe glory will come from the land."

Moses looks to the Son.[135]

"They will not understand that You, the Word, are the true beauty and glory."

Moses looks back to the land and laughs. It seems so small to him.

"No, I do not want that. You are my only friend; You are my only true love."

This is why the Three chose Moses. He wanted to see God's face more than anything else. Moses knows His name. God looks down on His friend and smiles. Moses feels the Spirit embrace him.

"Please, Father, take me home."

---

[133] Reference to 1 Corinthians 15:45–49.

[134] Deuteronomy 34:4 NLT

[135] Reference to Mark 9:4.

LOVE'S STRENGTH

A certain man of Zorah, named Manoah, from the clan of the Danites, had a wife who was childless, unable to give birth. The angel of the Lord appeared to her and said, "You are barren and childless, but you are going to become pregnant and give birth to a son. Now see to it that you drink no wine or other fermented drink and that you do not eat anything unclean. You will become pregnant and have a son whose head is never to be touched by a razor because the boy is to be a Nazirite, dedicated to God from the womb. He will take the lead in delivering Israel from the hands of the Philistines."

Judges 13:2-5

After putting him to sleep on her lap, she called for someone to shave off the seven braids of his hair... And his strength left him. Then she called, "Samson, the Philistines are upon you! He awoke from his sleep and thought, "I'll go out as before and shake myself free." But he did not know that the Lord had left him. Then the Philistines seized him, gouged out his eyes, and took him down to Gaza. Binding him with bronze shackles, they set him to grinding grain in the prison... Now the rulers of the Philistines assembled... to celebrate, saying, "Our god has delivered Samson, our enemy, into our hands." ...While they were in high spirits, they shouted, "Bring out Samson to entertain us." So they called Samson out of the prison, and he performed for them... Samson said to the servant who held his hand, "Put me where I can feel the pillars that support the *temple, so that I may lean against them." ... Then Samson prayed to the Lord, "Sovereign Lord, remember me. Please, God, strengthen me just once more, and let me with one blow get revenge on the Philistines for my two eyes." ... Samson said, "Let me die with the Philistines!" Then he pushed with all his might, and down came the temple on the rulers and all the people in it. Thus he killed many more when he died than while he lived.*

Judges 16:19-26,28-30

The righteous cry out, and the Lord hears them; He delivers them from all their troubles.

Psalm 34:17

I have swept away your offenses like a cloud, your sins like the morning mist. Return to me, for I have redeemed you.

Isaiah 44:22

No temptation has overtaken you except what is common to mankind. And God is faithful; he will not let you be tempted beyond what you can bear. But when you are tempted, he will also provide a way out so that you can endure it.

1 Corinthians 10:13

He once uprooted the gates that protected the city, and now he is cast in a dark prison in Gaza.[136] Once he was the greatest power Gaza had ever seen, and now Samson is just a slave, humiliated in his weakness.[137] Disgraced and blind, he is left with nothing to give.

---

[136] Reference to Judges 16:3. Prior to Samson being thrown in jail in Gaza, he destroyed the city gate.

[137] Reference to Judges 16:21. Samson was thrown in prison and forced to work as a slave grinding grain.

A prize to entertain the elite; he is called to come one last time. One last time, for them to disgrace Samson. One last time, for them to jeer and laugh at him. One last time, for them to mock God.

"Our god has delivered our enemy to us! The one who killed so many of us is now in our power! Bring out Samson so he can perform for us!"[138]

Samson is made to stand in shame in front of his enemies—in front of God's enemies. All sneering and ridiculing him. He has no strength any longer to feel pride. He just stands and feels the heat from their scoffing on his body. He has brought himself to this place. No one else is to blame for his shame. No one else betrayed him; he only betrayed himself.[139] He understands it was his own selfish pride that caused him to be blinded for so long. For years, he disobeyed because his eyes only looked upon his own lustful desires, and not on what God was commanding. For years, sin took his sight and caused him to see nothing else. He was blind long before the Philistines took his eyes.[140] Now that his eyes are gone, Samson can finally see the truth and the Lord's plan. In this moment, he is finally ready to obey. Samson is finally ready to give the Lord his heart completely.

Through the mocking and jeers, he asks the servant next to him for assistance.

"Place my hands against the two pillars. I want to rest against them."[141]

He raises his hands to feel the cold stone of the pillars under his fingertips. For so long, sin has kept him away from talking with the Father. Samson tried many times, but the Deceiver would come and whisper in his ear that he was not worthy, and Samson would stop. In the beginning, he felt so strong and powerful. His mother would tell him of the glory of his birth over and over again, preparing the way for his service

---

[138] Judges 16:24-25
[139] Reference to Delilah betraying him to the Philistines to be captured.
[140] Reference to Judges 16:21. The Philistines gouged out Samson's eyes when they captured him.
[141] Judges 16:26 NLT

to the Lord.[142] His mother would say that his life began with the blessing of God, and that blessing would lead him all of the days of his life. Now, standing here with his eyes gone, he thinks of how wrong his mother was. He failed that blessing. So far from grace Samson fell, that he cannot even remember the strength and confidence he once possessed.

Samson often wondered why God chose him. Samson reasoned it must have been a mistake because he was not capable of making things right; who is he to judge others?[143] Yahweh blessed Samson with the strength to lead His people to a path of righteousness. But Samson used his strength in vanity, and those he was called to judge ended up being the jury to the reckoning of his own justice here in this moment of ridicule.[144] Now after years of abusing it, his strength is gone and he is left weak. A pathetic toy used by his enemies to dishonor the God Samson was called to serve.

As Samson stands here in the circus of sin, feeling the cold stone pillars, he knows it is time to talk with his Father once more. He takes a deep breath, and utters his first prayer in years.

"O Lord..."

Samson's heart fills with the emotions he has pushed away for so many years.

"God..."

Samson does not understand how it is happening, but tears fill the empty, lifeless scars that were once his eyes.

"God, please remember me..."[145]

The tears begin to flow down his cheeks. The salty wet drops are the first humanity he has felt in his soul in a long time. They fill him with hope.

---

[142] Reference to Judges 13.

[143] God ordained Samson to be one of the judges of Israel.

[144] God blessed Samson with supernatural strength. Despite his strength, Samson was still captured by his enemy the Philistines and condemned by them.

[145] Judges 16:28 NLT

"Please Lord... please strengthen me just one more time..."[146]

He knows his whole life he has taken what he wanted without regard to what God wanted of him. Now it is time for that to stop.

"O God, give me strength, that I may be avenged on the Philistines for the loss of my two eyes."[147]

Samson is going to achieve justice—what he was called to do from his birth. The world stole everything from Samson: his birthright, his faith, his calling, and left him blinded for years. This is now his confession and plea for forgiveness of his sins. Not for his eyes now, for Samson is finally seeing for the first time, but for the twenty years that he lived for the world and not God.[148] Finally, Samson is ready to depend on God for his strength, not his own muscles and pride.

The Three look down upon him with love. The Son comes to the Father.

"He is My miracle. From the moment I announced his birth to his mother and father, his life was full of potential. Potential We ordained for him to achieve."[149]

"Yes," the Father answers.

"Then the Deceiver came to him. Came to him in so many different forms of pride, lust, greed, stubbornness, and vanity. He chose the world over and over again."

"Yes."

"He has not prayed to Us in years. He has burdened himself with shame, so much so that he let the weight of sin keep him from coming to Us. Through his guilt, he believes he no longer is worthy of a relationship with Us. Through his guilt, he has not lived up to his potential."

"Yes."

"He does not understand why he was chosen."

---

[146] Judges 16:28 NLT

[147] Judges 16:28 NLT

[148] Historians believe Samson's career as a judge lasted around twenty years.

[149] Reference to Judges 13:21-22. Some theologians believe the angel of the Lord was really Jesus.

"Yes."

"He does not understand that his obedience is not required for Our will to come to pass."

"Yes."

"And he does not understand that beyond all of the shame, disobedience, and sin he is still Our son, and We still love him."

"Yes."

"We are ready to fulfill his birthright."

"Yes."

"We are ready to bring him home to Us."

"Yes. I love him, and I want My son back."

The Father will give Samson His strength once more. The Father will not only fulfill His plan of showing the world that He is the only true God, but the Father will avenge those who stole His son away from Him for so many years. For so many years, the Father's heart has been breaking because Samson chose not to speak to Him. For so many years, the Father's heart has been crushed because Samson was blinded and could not see where his power was from. For so many years, the Father's heart has been torn because Samson loved the world more than Him. The Father wants His son back. The Father tells the Spirit to enter Samson one last time.

Samson feels a gust of the Spirit's breath enter his lungs. Samson lifts his head up and sees God's glory, and his eyes are no longer empty. Samson sees love for the first time. Samson's arms feel the power of the Spirit pulsing through them. For too long the Deceiver has controlled Samson's eyes, and now it is time for the Father to take them back.

It is the Father's anger against those who convinced Samson that he was not valuable that fills Samson's muscles with power. It is the Father's rage against the world who taught Samson that he was unworthy that causes Samson's posture to become strong, ready to bring the lies crashing down. It is the Father's fury at the Deceiver who tried to steal Samson from Him that gives Samson the glory to see the deceit crash once and for all.

The pillars come crashing down.

LOVE'S REDEMPTION

In the days when the judges ruled... a man of Bethlehem in Judah went to sojourn in the country of Moab, he and his wife and his two sons. The name of the man was Elimelek, and the name of his wife was Naomi... But Elimelek... died, and she was left with her two sons. These took Moabite wives; the name of the one was Orpah and the name of the other Ruth. They lived there about ten years, and both Mahlon and Chilion died, so that the woman was left without her two sons and her husband. Then she arose with her daughters-in-law to return from the country of Moab... But Naomi said to her two daughters-in-law, "Go, return each of you to her mother's house. May the Lord deal kindly with you, as you have dealt with the dead and with me. The Lord grant that you may find rest, each of you in the house of her husband!" Then she kissed them, and they lifted up their voices and wept. And they said to her, "No, we will return with you to your people." But Naomi said, "Turn back, my daughters... for it is exceedingly bitter to me for your sake that the hand of the Lord has gone out against me." Then they lifted up their voices and wept again. And Orpah kissed her mother-in-law, but Ruth clung to her... Ruth said, "Do not urge me to leave you or to return from following you. For where you go I will go, and where you lodge I will lodge. Your people shall be my people, and your God my God. Where you die I will die, and there will I be buried. May the Lord do so to me and more also if

anything but death parts me from you." And when Naomi saw that she was
determined to go with her, she said no more.

Ruth 1:1-6, 8-10, 12-14, 16-18

The Lord is near to the brokenhearted and saves the crushed in spirit.

Psalm 34:18

Blessed are those who mourn, for they shall be comforted.

Matthew 5:4

It has been ten years of death and disappointment, and Naomi has nothing left to give. It is time to go home—home to Israel. Naomi has never felt at home in Moab, this foreign land.[150] She has always known in her heart that this was not the place God wanted them to be. They tried to flee darkness only to find a new blackness that took everything away.[151] She knew there was nothing left in Israel for her either and she would be cast off to die. That was okay. She could no longer grieve, and welcomed her life ending.[152] Naomi is too exhausted to fight for the nothingness that her life has become. She is ready to go back and fade out.

She looks at her adopted daughters of this land with the last ounce of love she holds in her broken heart, and tells them to go back to their homes. She has nothing to give to them, and she can no longer be their mother. She is too tired. It is time for it all to end.

"No," they say. "We want to go with you to your people."[153]

She tries to seem touched by this display of loyalty and love, but she is not. She needs a release of the reminder of all she has lost. She tries to reason with them and show them that this is the only way,

---

[150] Moab was one of the nations that oppressed Israel during the time of Judges.
[151] Naomi's husband brought her to Moab to escape a famine in Israel.
[152] Naomi going back to Israel as a widow meant she would be homeless.
[153] Ruth 1:10 NLT

but they continue to insist. Naomi does not have the strength to be a mother any longer; the daughters need to go back. Finally, her broken, weary heart cannot take any more, and she yells out, "Things are far more *bitter* for me than for you, because the Lord, Himself, has raised His fist against me!"[154]

Finally, the words of her heart from the last ten years scream from her lips. Bitter. Naomi is bitter, she is angry, she is lost, and the Lord has caused it. For a moment she feels shame for allowing herself to say it out loud, but it feels good to cast the blame that has been secretly in her thoughts for years. The Lord has abandoned her. The Father has forgotten her. And now Naomi is bitter. She has been patient, giving the Lord ten years to make things better, and He has not. She has tried for ten years to see the beauty, but all she sees is her bitterness. For ten years, she has waited on the Lord to show her how all of this pain has a purpose, but He has not. For ten years, it has all been in vain and she is done waiting on the Lord.

Orpah relents and gives her mother one last embrace, but Ruth will not let go.

"Don't ask me to leave you and turn back. I will go wherever you go and live wherever you live. Your people will be my people, and your God will be my God. I will die where you die and will be buried there. May the Lord punish me severely if I allow anything but death to separate us."[155]

Naomi is not touched, but frustrated. She just wants to go home and quietly die. She wants to be with her husband and sons again. She needs them more than anything else. Her soul is screaming for release from this bondage from Ruth, but she quietly accepts defeat and their journey begins. The Lord has disappointed her yet again.

With every step of their journey, Naomi's bitterness grows. Bethlehem is coming close, and Naomi becomes nervous. She knows there will not be a welcome.

---

[154] Ruth 1:13 NLT
[155] Reference to Ruth 1:16.

Home finally finds Naomi. With stares and shock, the people judge her as she approaches. The women come to see her, and are stunned by the shattered shell standing before them instead of the confident woman they once knew.[156]

"Is it really Naomi?" they question.[157] "Don't call me Naomi," she tells them. "Instead, call me Mara, for the Almighty has made life very bitter for me.[158] I went away full, but the Lord has brought me home empty. Why should you call me Naomi when the Lord has caused me to suffer, and the Almighty has sent such tragedy?"[159]

Naomi wants all to know that it is the Lord who cast her off, who turned His back on her long ago. There is nothing to rejoice over; this is not a happy homecoming but an ending. With that, Naomi succumbs to a life—fitting to a pathetic casualty like her—of gleaning.[160] She prays that the food will be scarce, and her stomach will stay empty, and it will not take long to end all of this pain.

Then Ruth insists on gathering with her. Naomi sees all that she gathers—too much for Ruth's arms to carry. Why? Why did the farmer allow such a thing? This is not supposed to happen. They are the lowest of the low; why are they getting blessings now? Blessings that Naomi does not want.

"So much!" Naomi exclaimed. "Where did you gather all this grain today? Where did you work?"[161]

Naomi catches Ruth's surprised look, not understanding the annoyed tone in her voice. Naomi tries to correct her attitude.

"May the Lord bless the one who helped you."[162]

---

[156] Ruth 1:19 NLT

[157] Ruth 1:19 NLT

[158] Mara means "bitter."

[159] Ruth 1:20-21 NLT

[160] Gleaning was done by the poor in the village. They were allowed to take the leftover grain from the fields after the harvest. People who gleaned were looked down upon.

[161] Ruth 2:19 NLT

[162] Ruth 2:19 NLT

Ruth, reassured by Naomi's change in her tone, goes on to tell her mother-in-law how a man named Boaz allowed her to gather in his fields. Naomi's demeanor instantly changes at the sound of Boaz's name. She feels a warm conviction in her heart. To her surprise, she is genuinely touched.

"May the Lord bless him! He is showing his kindness to us as well as your dead husband. That man is one of our closest relatives, one of our family redeemers."

Redeemer echoes in Naomi's ears. Could Boaz help her?

Ruth is so excited by Naomi's reaction that she continues on with her good news.

"What's more, Boaz even told me to come back and stay with his harvesters until the entire harvest is completed."[163]

Naomi's mind begins to plot.

"This is wonderful! Do as he said. Stay with his workers right through the whole harvest. You will be safe there, unlike in other fields."[164]

Naomi decides right then that Boaz will be her redeemer. Not for herself, but for Ruth. She wants Boaz to accept Ruth into his family so she can then let go and die in her bitterness. She plots all throughout the harvest until her plan is set. Then she takes it to Ruth.

"My daughter, it's time that I found a permanent home for you, so that you will be provided for. Boaz is a close relative of ours, and he's been very kind by letting you gather grain with his workers..."[165]

As she speaks, Ruth becomes shocked and embarrassed by Naomi's plan. The plan is not in Ruth's heart, but she can see Naomi is desperate and wants to honor her. So, with love in her heart for Naomi, Ruth answers her call.

---

[163] Ruth 2:21 NLT
[164] Reference to Ruth 2:22.
[165] Ruth 3:1-2 NLT

"I will do everything you say."[166]

Ruth obeys everything Naomi instructs her to do, and soon Boaz is trapped. Boaz is not angry at Ruth, but feels compassion for her. He knows this is not of her doing, but comes from a daughter's heart that is pure, wanting to please her mother. Boaz carefully weighs out the situation and tries his best to be a man honoring of God. In the end, Boaz knows the Father is calling him to be the redeemer of this family. Not to redeem only Ruth, but also to redeem Naomi.

Boaz goes to the town gate, gives away his sandal, and makes Ruth his bride.[167] The witnesses exclaim with praises and shouts, "May the Lord make the woman who is now coming into your house like Rachel and Leah, from whom all the nation of Israel descended! May you be great... and famous in Bethlehem. And may the Lord give you descendants by this young woman who will be like those of our ancestor Perez, the son of Tamar and Judah."[168]

Boaz brings Ruth to his home, and insists Naomi join them as well. Naomi tries to stay away. This is not her plan; this is not what she wants. She wants to go back to gleaning, and be done with it all. Boaz will not allow this, and her story continues on, much to her disappointment.

Naomi stopped praying to the Father years ago. She has been angry for so long; she does not know another feeling. She has played the part of devoted follower so well, no one knows her secret. She puts on the disguise of faith and walks out into the world, but inside she has been yelling at the Father for ten years. The Father took everything away from her that she loved. He took everything she needed to live, and then He left her too. She never felt His comfort or peace, so she stopped asking for His love. Naomi knows all the right words to say to keep people at

---

[166] Ruth 3:5 NLT

[167] Men met at the town gate to handle business transactions. Marrying and taking responsibility for a widow was considered a transaction called "redeeming." To seal the business deal, a man would take off his sandal and hand it over to the other men.

[168] Ruth 4:11-12 NLT

bay and make them believe that she still knows the Father. She does not know anymore if she still believes in the words she preaches to others, but she knows she no longer feels them in her heart. She has not felt anything beyond her grief for ten years. Now Boaz wants her to feel something more again and will not let her just die. She is in his home and has no gratitude for it. She decides to make another plan... but then... Ruth.

"Mother, I am with child."

Ruth glows with a renewed happiness that Naomi has not seen on her daughter-in-law's face since her son was alive.

"Please, Mother, stay with me. I cannot do this without you."

Does Ruth know of her plan? Is she trying to guilt Naomi to stay?

"I love you, Mother."

Once again, Naomi is trapped. Why is this girl forcing herself to be her daughter? Why is she honoring her, Naomi questions? She stays with Ruth and Boaz, but refuses to open her heart and let go of the bitterness. She begins to plan again. She plots that the moment the baby is here, she will leave and finally find her peace.

Long months pass, and finally it is time for the child to come. Naomi is ready with her plan and counts the hours. She is in the room, along with the midwives, and memories keep flooding her mind. She can remember the screams of pain she had when birthing her sons. She remembers the first time she looked upon them. She can remember them lying on her chest and knowing instinctively that she was their mother. These memories suffocate her and she cannot breathe. Naomi looks down upon Ruth, seeing the sweat on her brow and the tension in her face as she struggles with the pain too. Naomi flees.

She runs out of the room. She feels her lungs collapsing. She falls to her knees. Naomi does not know if she is praying or crying. It is all too raw to name it, but for the first time in ten years she does not feel anger. She is hyperventilating, but manages to get the words out...

"Yahweh, I do not know what to say. I do not have anything to say; I am just empty. I have been empty for so long. I am scared... please come to me now!"

She cannot control her shaking or her hysterical tears. It has been ten years, and finally she has broken. Her subdued moans become piercing wails.

"Come to me now! I cannot breathe! I am going to die if you do not!"

A commanding voice comes.

"Daughter, stop."

Naomi is paralyzed and does not move.

"Daughter..."

Naomi is too weak to say anything. The Spirit comes and sits with her.

"Daughter... stop... breathe Me in now."

Naomi has no more fight left in her. She has no more plans. She is ready to breathe again, so she takes a deep breath. It hurts though. The voice of the Spirit becomes soft.

"Breathe again, slowly. It will stop hurting soon."

"You took everything away from me."

"No."

"Yes, You took my husband and my sons."

"They were never yours. They were My children."

"I do not like that answer."

"I know."

"I am not capable of distinguishing the difference... They were mine... I held them... I loved them..."

"I know."

"Then how can You expect me to understand and survive this grief?"

"I do not expect it."

Naomi becomes angry.

"Well then, why me? Why did You give it to me?"

"I did not give you anything. Death is in this world. It was not My doing, but it is here. Now My children have to experience it. But I never expect My children to experience it alone. Grief is too big for you to carry; I want to carry it for you."

"But You have left me! You have never comforted me or carried my grief at all!"

"Daughter, I have made you wake up every day. I have not allowed the grief to kill you. I gave you a daughter to love and support you. I have loved you, even though you have cursed Me in your heart. I have been waiting for ten years for you to call out to Me so I can do more."

"I had nothing in me to call out to You. All I have is the bitterness."

"I know; that is why I have continued taking care of you."

"There was a time I could not see anything beyond my love for You... But for the last ten years all I have seen is the grief and bitterness." Naomi pauses and allows the tears to fall from her eyes. "Even though I do not want You there, You still have not left my heart."

"I know I have not left your heart."

"No, You have not. Even though I want to deny You, I have not been able to. But I have been so angry at You."

"That is okay. You are allowed to be angry. I still love you. You will always be My daughter. Your story is not over; allow Me to end your grief. Your husband and sons are with Me worshipping, and I need you to worship Me now and raise this baby."

"I do not know if I can do it. It feels so long until I can see my husband and sons again. Time is not in weeks or even days, but in minutes. The minutes feel like slow torture holding me in a state of pain and grief. I do not want to wait any longer. I want to see them now more than I want a new life."

"Not a new life, but a continuation. All I have wanted to do these past ten years is love you and fill you with My breath. I have been waiting outside of your heart for the moment you would allow Me to enter. If you can allow Me to love you now, then I will give you the reasons to worship again. You are a part of My plan. This new baby is My chosen child, and he will provide a way for the Son.[169] You will be his grandmother, and you will guide him. He will bring you joy and make the time until you see your sons again go quickly. He is your comfort until that day comes."

---

[169] Ruth's son became the grandfather to King David.

Before Naomi can think, she hears Ruth scream. For the first time Naomi feels a mother's instinct for Ruth. Her daughter is screaming in pain. Ruth is her daughter, whom she loves. God has provided for her over the past ten years. She needs to help her daughter now. Naomi has a breath and strength in her lungs that she has not felt in ten years. Her legs feel the urgency, and she pulls herself up. Naomi runs back into the room to be with Ruth. She will trust God to serve her now.

Naomi looks down upon the baby and falls immediately in love. He is perfect. He will bring Naomi comfort. Naomi holds him in her arms and her bitterness leaves her. The women in the room, the other mothers, gather around her and encourage Naomi.

"Praise the Lord who has given you a family redeemer today! May he be famous in Israel. May this child restore your youth and care for you in your old age. For he is the son of your daughter-in-law who loves you so much and who has been better to you than seven sons!"[170]

Naomi feels peace. Naomi feels comforted. She no longer carries her grief alone. She takes care of the baby as if he was her own.[171] She has allowed God to give her hope and love, and now she can worship. She is the grandmother of Obed.[172]

---

[170] Ruth 4:13–15 NLT
[171] Reference to Ruth 4:16.
[172] Obed means "to serve and to worship" in Hebrew.

LOVE'S PSALM

Psalms 6, 9, 18, 13, 22, 25, 23, 27, 55, 69, 143,145
But now your kingdom will not endure; the Lord has sought out a man after
his own heart and appointed him ruler of his people, because you have not kept
the Lord's command.

1 Samuel 13:14

After removing Saul, he made David their king. God testified concerning
him: "I have found David, son of Jesse, a man after my own heart; he will do
everything I want him to do."

Acts 13:22

Praise be to the God and Father of our Lord Jesus Christ! In his great mercy
he has given us new birth into a living hope through the resurrection of Jesus
Christ from the dead, and into an inheritance that can never perish, spoil, or
fade. This inheritance is kept in heaven for you, who through faith are shield-
ed by God's power until the coming of the salvation… In all this you greatly
rejoice, though now for a little while you may have had to suffer grief in all
kinds of trials. These have come so that the proven genuineness of your faith—
of greater worth than gold, which perishes even though refined by fire—may
result in praise, glory, and honor when Jesus Christ is revealed. Though you

have not seen him, you love him; and even though you do not see him now, you
believe in him and are filled with an inexpressible and glorious joy, for you
are receiving the end result of your faith, the salvation of your souls.

1 Peter 1:3-9

David falls to his knees. Dawn is approaching soon. He has been up all night. There are too many emotions to feel, and he cannot express all that is within him. He longs for God's heart; it is what he craves, but he still feels the pain. Pain from his own wrongdoing and from those around him. He does not understand his world, and no longer knows what to pray for. All he understands is his confusion and heartache.

"O Lord, why do You stand so far away?" His voice becomes a silent whisper. "Why do You hide when I am in trouble?"[173]

David feels only reverence as he tries to reach his Father. He needs to explain his grief; he needs his Father's rescue.

"O Lord, do not rebuke me in Your anger or discipline me in Your rage. Have compassion on me, Lord, for I am weak."[174] His voices cracks and he repeats, "I am weak... so weak."

He feels so exhausted and alone. He has tried over and over to be what the Lord has asked of him, but over and over he has failed. It has been a lifetime set on repeat. Every season brings a new trial and a new way to sin. David starts over, every time on fire, burning for the Lord's approval, and then slowly falls. A lifetime of moments blurred together. Does it matter what trial it is at this moment? How is the pain from last season's winter different than this season's spring? It all adds up to the consequence of pain. Is life not just a long prayer of asking for God's rescue? All David wants is to be delivered from this trouble. Once again to be delivered. But he feels sick in his mind, sick in his soul, and sick in his heart.

---

[173] Psalm 10:1 NLT
[174] Psalm 6:1-2 NLT

"Heal me, Lord, for my body is in agony. I am sick at heart."[175]

He feels abandoned. He has been praying this prayer for so long it seems.

"How long, O Lord, until You restore me? Return, O Lord, and rescue me. Save me because of Your unfailing love."[176]

Yes, David's heart worships... His unfailing love. The Father loves him; David feels it and he knows it. Why then does he still cry? Why is it that David's tears are his only comfort right now? He is trying to move forward so he does not drown in his tears, but they keep coming, weighing him further and further down.

"I am worn out from sobbing..."[177]

David tries to take a breath, but the sob in his throat catches.

"All night I flood my bed with weeping, drenching it with my tears." A brief surge of energy fills him, and David screams out to Yahweh: "My vision is blurred by grief; my eyes are worn out because of all my enemies."[178]

David's body begins to shake, and his vision is becoming obscure. His emotions are overtaking his wits. He is beginning to feel the exhaustion of pleading with the Lord throughout the night.

"Listen to my prayer, O God. Do not ignore my cry for help! Please listen and answer me, for I am overwhelmed by my troubles... My heart is in anguish. The terror of death overpowers me. Fear and trembling overwhelm me. I cannot stop shaking. Oh, how I wish I had wings like a dove; then I would fly far away and rest! I would fly far away to the quiet of the wilderness; how quickly I would escape far away from this wild storm of hatred."[179]

David's body gives out and he falls upon his face crying. He cries out his soul completely. David holds nothing back; he releases it all to

---

[175] Psalm 6:2-3 NLT
[176] Psalm 6:3-4 NLT
[177] Psalm 6:6 NLT
[178] Psalm 6:6-7 NLT
[179] Psalm 55:1-8 NLT

the Father. He lies there as the minutes bring new colors to the sky. He has lost all track of the time he has spent in prayer. Looking out the window, he sees the sun kissing the sky and is confused; was he not just in darkness? Did God let a new day come again without ending his suffering? *How could He?* David screams inside of himself.

"No! No, not again. Not another day!" He cannot stomach another day.

Then a new rush of energy fills him. He becomes desperate. He becomes frustrated... He becomes angry. David stands in protest. He stands in rebellion, and he yells at his Father.

"O Lord, how long will You forget me? Forever? How long will You look the other way? How long must I struggle with anguish in my soul, with sorrow in my heart... every day? How long will my enemy have the upper hand?"[180]

Why does the Father not answer him? David becomes angrier. He lifts his hands up, shakes his fists at the Lord, and demands an answer.

"Turn and answer me, O Lord my God! Restore the light to my eyes, or I will die! Don't let my enemies gloat, saying, 'We have defeated him!' Don't let them rejoice at my downfall."[181]

David feels like his words are falling onto deaf ears, so he tries to convince the Father once more, and yells louder.

"I trust in Your unfailing love. I will rejoice because You have rescued me. I will sing to the Lord because He has been so good to me."[182]

He wonders if that convinces the Lord to answer his plea. He waits for a response, but only silence comes. He screams out in desperation.

"My God, My God! Why have You forsaken me? Why do You remain so distant? Why do You ignore my cries for help?"[183]

Silence.

---

[180] Psalm 13:1-2 NLT
[181] Psalm 13:3-4 NLT
[182] Psalm 13:5-6 NLT
[183] Reference to Psalm 22:1

"Please... answer me. Every day I call to You, my God, but You do not answer. Every night You hear my voice, but I find no relief... You have been my God from the moment I was born. Do not stay so far from me, for trouble is near and no one else can help me. My enemies surround me like a herd of bulls... like roaring lions attacking their prey, they come at me with open mouths."[184]

David stops. He looks around at the emptiness that surrounds him. He lets out a sigh, and his voice becomes softer. He remembers when he was a child in the fields singing out to the Lord. It was there the Spirit came to him, and turned David's love for the Father into a calling on his life. Why? Why this calling? Why him? David's love for the Father has not been enough, because the Lord has continued to allow him to feel the pain. He falls back down onto the floor, curls his lifeless soul into a ball, and quietly talks out into the emptiness.

"My life is poured out like water, and all my bones are out of joint. My heart is like wax melting within me."[185] His voices cracks. "My strength has dried up like sunbaked clay. My tongue sticks to the roof of my mouth. You have laid me in the dust and left me for dead."[186]

He lies there, confused in the minutes. What does it matter—nothing has come except the silence still. The silence is too loud and it fills him again with rage. David jumps up and shouts out.

"O Lord, do not stay away! You are my strength; come quickly to my aid! Rescue me from a violent death; spare my precious life from these dogs. Snatch me from the lions' jaws, and from the horns of these wild oxen."[187]

David reaches out his arms wide, and is ready for the Lord to pour down on him, but no rain comes. He falls again to his knees. His body

---

[184] Psalm 22:2, 10-13 NLT
[185] Psalm 22:14 NLT
[186] Psalm 22:15 NLT
[187] Psalm 22:19-21 NLT

feels defeated. He does not even have the strength to let the tears fall. His voice is gone, and he can barely whisper.

"Save me, O God, for the floodwaters are up to my neck. Deeper and deeper I sink into the mire; I can't find a foothold to stand on. I am in deep water, and the floods overwhelm me. I am exhausted from crying for help; my throat is parched and dry. My eyes are swollen with weeping, waiting for my God to help me... But I keep right on praying to You, Lord, hoping this is the time You will show me favor. In Your unfailing love, O God, answer my prayer with Your sure salvation. Pull me out of the mud; don't let me sink any deeper! Rescue me from those who hate me, and pull me from these deep waters. Don't let the floods overwhelm me, or the deep waters swallow me, or the pit of death devour me. Answers my prayers, O Lord, for Your unfailing love is wonderful. Turn and take care of me; for Your mercy is so plentiful... I am suffering and in pain. Rescue me, O God, by Your saving power."[188]

David stops. He is too tired to continue. He watches the sun rise higher in the sky. He listens to the birds fly above him. He looks out at the land and marvels at creation. He is still for a long time. David is waiting for the Father to send His Spirit. He never feels the Spirit come. With a soul full of faith, David chases after the Lord's heart one last time.

"Hear my prayer, O Lord; listen to my plea! Answer me because You are faithful and righteous... My enemy has chased me. He has knocked me to the ground. He forces me to live in darkness like those in the grave. I am losing all hope; I am paralyzed with fear... I reach out for You. I thirst for You as parched land thirsts for rain. Come quickly, Lord, and answer me, for my depression deepens. Don't turn away from me or I will die. Let me hear of Your unfailing love to me in the morning, for I am trusting You. Show me where to walk, for I have come to You in prayer. Save me from my enemies, Lord; I run to You to hide me. Teach me to do Your will, for You are my God. May Your gracious Spirit lead

---

[188] Psalm 69:1-3, 13-16, 29 NLT

me forward on a firm footing. For the glory of Your name, O Lord, save me. In Your righteousness, bring me out of this distress. In Your unfailing love, cut off all my enemies and destroy all my foes." He allows the tears to fall. "For I am Your servant."[189]

The Spirit comes down upon David and whispers into his ear.

"The Father loves you because you are full of repentance, not sin. The sin comes and goes, but your heart of true repentance never waivers. That is the heart the Father can use to change the world. That is the heart the Father will use for His plan. That is why you were chosen."

The Spirit shows David the plan—a vision that leaves David prostrated in awe. Unworthy as David is, the Father has a greater purpose for his pain, and he needs to march onward. David understands now that darkness will fade and there will be a time when only the Light will remain. The Son will come to end the darkness once and for all. The Spirit tells David to speak of the vision he has just seen, and to believe. David slowly utters the words,

"Eli, Eli, lema sabachthani."[190]

David sees the Son crying those words out into the darkness. David sees the plan, like a play acted out for him. David realizes now that he has never been alone. The Father has always been with him. The Father will answer his cry, along with the entire world's, through the Son. The Spirit tells David to continue to speak out the vision he is seeing.

"My God, my God, why have you forsaken me?"[191]

The Spirit continues on, and David speaks of what he is witnessing.

"My enemies surround me like a pack of dogs; an evil gang closes in on me. They have pierced my hands and feet. I can count every bone in my body. My enemies stare at me and gloat. They divide my clothes among themselves and throw dice for my garments."[192]

---

[189] Psalm 143:1-12 NLT
[190] Matthew 27:46 NLT
[191] Matthew 27:46 NLT
[192] Psalm 22:16-18 NLT

David sees the greatest suffering of all. He sees the Lamb. Quiet tears roll down his cheeks. He does not understand why the Father chose him to be part of the plan. He is humbled by the Father's pain. The Spirit fills David, and he has peace. David stays on his knees with his head cast down. This is a holy moment. This is the moment he understands true love.

"I will praise You, Lord, with all my heart. I will tell of all the marvelous things You have done. I will be filled with joy because of You. I will sing praises to Your name, O Most High."[193]

David looks up with tears filling his eyes. He raises his hands in praise.

"I love You, Lord; You are my strength. The Lord is my rock, my fortress, and my savior; my God is my rock, in whom I find protection. He is my shield, the strength of my salvation, and my stronghold... The ropes of death surrounded me; the floods of destruction swept over me... But in my distress I cried out to the Lord; yes, I prayed to my God for help. He heard me from His sanctuary; my cry reached his ears... He reached down from heaven and rescued me; He drew me out of deep waters. He delivered me from my powerful enemies, from those who hated me and were too strong for me. They attacked me at the moment when I was weakest, but the Lord upheld me. He led me to a place of safety; He rescued me because He delights in me..."[194]

David becomes excited and jumps to his feet. He cannot contain the joy.

"To you, O Lord, I lift up my soul. I trust in You, my God!... Show me the path where I should walk, O Lord; point out the right road for me to follow. Lead me by Your faith and teach me, for You are the God who saves me. All day long I put my hope in You. The Lord is good and does what is right; He shows the proper path to those who go astray... The Lord leads with unfailing love and faithfulness..."[195]

---

[193] Psalm 9:1-2 NLT
[194] Psalm 18:1-19 NLT
[195] Psalm 25:1-8, 10 NLT

David looks out into the world that has been causing his pain, and he realizes how foolish he has been. He finds new delight in it. David sees how beautiful creation truly is.

"The Lord is my light and my salvation—so why should I be afraid? The Lord protects me from danger—so why should I tremble? When evil people come to destroy me... my heart will know no fear. Even if they attack me, I remain confident... For He will conceal me when troubles come; He will hide me in His sanctuary. He will place me out of reach on a high rock. Then I will hold my head high; above my enemies who surround me."[196]

David has beautiful clarity of his Father's love for him. He breathes it in, and fills his lungs with the sweet Spirit. He sits; his body feels no more pain and his muscles are relaxed.

"The Lord is my shepherd; I shall not be in want. He lets me rest in green pastures; He leads me beside still waters. He renews my strength. He guides me along right paths, bringing honor to His name. Even when I walk through the shadows of the valley of death, I will fear no evil, for you are close beside me. Your rod and Your staff protect and comfort me. You prepare a feast for me in the presence of my enemies. You welcome me as a guest, anointing my head with oil. My cup overflows with bless-ings. Surely Your goodness and unfailing love will pursue me all the days of my life, and I will live in the house of the Lord forever."[197]

David looks to his Father. David does not have all of the answers; and he knows confusion will still plague him, but he knows the Father's love and trusts in Him. That will be his comfort for always.

"I will exalt You, my God and King, and bless Your name forever and ever. I will praise You every day, and I will praise You forever... I will meditate on Your majestic, glorious splendor and Your wonderful miracles... I will proclaim Your greatness."[198]

---

[196] Psalm 27:1-6 NLT
[197] Psalm 23:1-6 NLT
[198] Psalm 145:1-6 NLT

LOVE'S DALET

King Nebuchadnezzar made an image of gold... Then the herald loudly proclaimed, "Nations and peoples of every language, this is what you are commanded to do: As soon as you hear the sound of the horn, flute, zither, lyre, harp, pipe, and all kinds of music, you must fall down and worship the image of gold that King Nebuchadnezzar has set up. Whoever does not fall down and worship will immediately be thrown into a blazing furnace." ... At this time some astrologers came forward and denounced the Jews. They said to King Nebuchadnezzar... "Your Majesty has issued a decree that everyone who hears the sound... of music must fall down and worship the image of gold and that whoever does not fall down and worship will be thrown into a blazing furnace. But there are some Jews whom you have set over the affairs of the province of Babylon—Shadrach, Meshach, and Abednego—who pay no attention to you, Your Majesty. They neither serve your gods nor worship the image of gold you have set up." Furious with rage, Nebuchadnezzar summoned Shadrach, Meshach, and Abednego... and Nebuchadnezzar said to them, "Is it true, Shadrach, Meshach, and Abednego, that you do not serve my gods or worship the image of gold I have set up... Shadrach, Meshach, and Abednego replied to him, "King Nebuchadnezzar, we do not need to defend ourselves before you in this matter. If we are thrown into the blazing furnace, the God we serve is able to deliver us from it, and he will deliver us from Your Majesty's hand. But even if he does not, we want you to know, Your Majesty,

that we will not serve your gods or worship the image of gold you have set up."
Then Nebuchadnezzar was furious with Shadrach, Meshach, and Abed-
nego, and his attitude toward them changed. He ordered the furnace heated
seven times hotter than usual and commanded some of the strongest soldiers in
his army to tie up Shadrach, Meshach, and Abednego and throw them into
the blazing furnace.

Daniel 3:1, 4-6, 8-14, 16-20

When you pass through the waters, I will be with you; and when you pass
through the rivers, they will not sweep over you. When you walk through the
fire, you will not be burned; the flames will not set you ablaze. For I am the
Lord your God, the Holy One of Israel, your Savior.

Isaiah 43:2-3

Blessed is the one who perseveres under trial because, having stood the test,
that person will receive the crown of life that the Lord has promised to those
who love him.

James 1:12

Dear friends, do not be surprised at the fiery ordeal that has come on you to test
you, as though something strange were happening to you. But rejoice inasmuch
as you participate in the sufferings of Christ, so that you may be overjoyed when
his glory is revealed. If you are insulted because of the name of Christ, you are
blessed, for the Spirit of glory and of God rests on you.

1 Peter 4:12-14

The order comes to the Soldier, and he is astonished. What rage has caused this demand? He does not question it, but obeys, and gathers more wood to make the blaze hotter. He looks for dry wood that will ignite the furnace into a cataclysmic firestorm. The flames grow from reds and yellows to electric ice blues and greens. The Soldier knows these flames are too great, and they will consume deep down to a person's soul.

He gazes into the deep pit with layers of wood, coals, and bones—a holocaust of memories. A ramp enters the pit, stained with the footprints of those who have gone before.[199] The Soldier knows that this time it is different. The heat from the pit makes him feel sick to his stomach. The heat radiating from his armor is causing his skin to turn red, but it is not warm enough to stop his shaking. The Soldier's bones feel cold. He feels unrest in his body, like a fever of death. The Soldier's confusion grows and he knows he has to get away from this pit. The heat is suffocating him. He wants to run from the flames; he has had enough of the death and desperately wants to escape. He knows nothing good can come from the fire.

The king takes his place high above to watch the spectacle. His eyes grow big when he sees the pit. His breath catches, and he questions what he has done. The flames are too great; the fire is out of control. Panic sets in as the king thinks, "*What has his rage caused? Why did my fury need to be quenched seven times over?*"[200] But it is too late; the prisoners enter, tied and bound. When the king sees their faces, he becomes frightened. The prisoners have peace on their faces. They walk at a calm pace. The king looks up and knows to be scared of the Father who brings that peace.

The Soldier looks to the king and feels panic. He steps back into the shadows as the prisoners walk toward the pit. Other soldiers are guiding them and their footsteps become slower and hesitant. None of the soldiers want to continue—something in their spirits is telling them to stop. The soldiers do not want to approach the ramp; they do not have hope. Each step brings them closer to their own judgment. As they step onto the head of the ramp, the flames engulf them. The Soldier, hidden in the shadows, watches as his fellow soldiers

---

[199] Historians believe the furnace had a ramp that the prisoners used to enter.

[200] This is a reference to Daniel 3:13, 19

die from the judgment of the flames. There is no one left forcing the prisoners ahead, but the prisoners still move forward. Alone, the three walk into the fire of their own accord. No fear, just faith guides their steps. The Soldier is struggling to find his breath—he does not know if it is from the smoke or his shock. What is he witnessing? Then the ropes on the prisoners burn away, allowing their escape, but they continue to walk on into the pit. The Soldier is filled with awe and fear.

The three are not without fear. They are not without trepidation. They are not without confusion. The anticipation of the fire has been a heavy burden, causing excoriating turmoil in their hearts. The hours have felt like years. They do not know how their salvation will come, but they have faith, and that faith cooled the fire. It is their faith that told them to continue to walk down the ramp.

As the three reach the bottom of the ramp, they pause, then suddenly begin to enter the pit. They seem to be running into the pit. The Soldier squints to look, and then falls to his knees at the sight. There is another Man in the pit! How can that be? Who is this Man? The Soldier does not understand. He looks around for assurance that others are seeing it too—assurance he does not need. He looks up to the king as he hears him shout out, and tears begin to fall from the king's eyes. They all know. There are four men in that pit.

No one dares to move. All is holy and sacred. It does not need to be explained—the Spirit has come and opened all of their eyes. The Soldier looks down at his feet and knows they are not worthy to stand on the same ground as the Lord. The Soldier knows the Son is with the three in the pit.

With a triumphant blaze, the Son stands in the middle of the fire. What a beautiful sight He is. In the midst of the flames is His glory. The Soldier watches as the three run to Him and begin to worship. He feels a pain of jealousy in his heart. The Soldier wishes he, too, could be in the pit worshipping. The Soldier sees this was not a fire of destruction, but one of holy deliverance.

It is a pit designed by the enemy to destroy everything. To rob one of hope. It is a fire so great, there seems to be no way to survive it. But then, a fourth Man enters. Outside there are only three, but inside the fire the fourth is there. The fourth came when the three needed Him the most. The Soldier wishes he had a rescuer like that. What others see as his life is the Soldier's all-consuming pit. Bottomless and without hope, with no one to calm the flames for him.

The Soldier is awakened from his daydream when he hears the Son call the three to come to Him. He longs for the Son to call to him as well, but he just stands in the shadows watching this miracle. The Soldier hears the Son tell the three that He will protect them from the flames. He will turn this fire into a cleansing kiln that will produce a great masterpiece. The Son gives the three peace and hope. Then the Son talks about a plan. "What plan?" the Soldier's heart cries out. He wants to be part of a plan too.

The Soldier watches as the three and the Son embrace. The four talk together like old friends. The Soldier hears the Son speak of a love that no fire can incinerate. The prisoners are surviving and the flames are not burning them at all. The Soldier realizes the three were never the prisoners, but he was. The three received the privilege of going into the fire to reach the fourth. A fire pit designed for no escape just revealed a dalet—the Son. He is the door of escape out of the fire.[201]

The Soldier watches the fourth walk the three out of the pit. As the three reach the top of the ramp they seem renewed and stronger. Tears come rushing down the Soldier's cheeks. His heart cries out...

"Why could that not have been me?"

---

[201] Dalet is the Hebrew word for four, and it also means "door."

LOVE'S GUARDIAN

Now Daniel so distinguished himself... by his exceptional qualities that the king planned to set him over the whole kingdom... administrators and satraps went as a group to the king and said:" May King Darius live forever... the king should issue an edict and enforce the decree that anyone who prays to any god or human being during the next thirty days, except to you, Your Majesty, shall be thrown into the lions' den..." So King Darius put the decree in writing. Now when Daniel learned that the decree had been published, he went home to his upstairs room where the windows opened toward Jerusalem. Three times a day he got down on his knees and prayed, giving thanks to his God, just as he had done before. Then these men went as a group and found Daniel praying and asking God for help. So they went to the king and spoke to him about his royal decree... "Daniel, who is one of the exiles from Judah, pays no attention to you, Your Majesty, or to the decree you put in writing. He still prays three times a day." When the king heard this, he was greatly distressed; he was determined to rescue Daniel and made every effort until sundown to save him. Then the men went as a group to King Darius and said to him, "Remember, Your Majesty, that according to the law of the Medes and Persians no decree or edict that the king issues can be changed." So the king gave the order, and they brought Daniel and threw him into the lions' den. The king said to Daniel, "May your God, whom you serve continually, rescue you!" A stone was brought and placed over the mouth of the den, and the king sealed it with

his own signet ring and with the rings of his nobles, so that Daniel's situation might not be changed... At the first light of dawn, the king got up and hurried to the lions' den. When he came near the den, he called to Daniel in an anguished voice, "Daniel, servant of the living God, has your God, whom you serve continually, been able to rescue you from the lions?" Daniel answered, "May the king live forever! My God sent his angel, and he shut the mouths of the lions. They have not hurt me, because I was found innocent in his sight. Nor have I ever done any wrong before you, Your Majesty."

Daniel 6:3-22

Never will I leave you; never will I forsake you. So we can say with confidence, the Lord is my helper; I will not be afraid. What can mere mortals do to me?

Hebrews 13:5-6

I know your deeds. See, I have placed before you an open door that no one can shut. I know that you have little strength, yet you have kept my word and have not denied my name.

Revelation 3:8

Daniel cannot see them, but he knows they are there. He can feel their presence. Daniel keeps his movements to a minimum, not because of fear, but to show respect. How many are there, he wonders? Do they look the same as in his dreams? If he reaches out, can he touch them? Daniel knows he has never been in a more holy place.

He stretches his old shoulders.[202] Time has aged his body; the young boy who first entered this land is now an old man. The push into this den has been going on for seventy years, causing cuts, bruises, and scars; he wonders if he has the years left to see them heal. It was

---

[202] Historians believe Daniel was in his eighties when he was thrown into the pit.

never a question of if he would go into the den, but when he would go into the den.

A cage full of hungry lions, forced to live in captivity to kill for revenge of man's law. Man's answer to justice. Man's answer to sin. The lions are not the feared enemy; they are just cats needing to be fed. It's man's heart that should be feared. Daniel knows this. He looks to the lions, sees their majestic bodies, and praises God for His beautiful creation. From their paws to their commanding roar, these animals are the image of God's glory.

How many does it take to keep their mouths shut, Daniel wonders? Do the lions become kittens to their touch or do they have to use force to tame the lion's instincts? Do the lions see them or just feel their spiritual caress? He squints harder, but still does not see them. Daniel bows his head in reverence and honors the heavenly event that is happening right now. He feels God's love wash over him.

From the moment Daniel stepped into this foreign land, he has asked God to take him back home. God's answer was always "wait." So Daniel waited. He has waited most of his life. He has never understood why he was chosen. God marked him as chosen from his boyhood. Daniel has strived to honor that calling, and has done everything in his power to obey the Lord. He has worked endlessly over and over again. He has served king after king, always bringing glory to the Lord, but always waiting. Waiting to enter the den. Daniel knew that the den was the only way home.[203]

In Daniel's waiting, the Lord gave him dreams. Dreams that would keep him up for days, dreams that would bring peace and hope, and dreams that would seem so far out of reach. Why was he the one chosen to have these dreams? He never understood that, but he understood what the dreams meant and what was coming. He knew God's plan. The plan of love.

---

[203] Historians believe it was shortly after the lions' den that Daniel finally returned to Israel.

The den is not part of God's plan, but of man's. Sin created the den. The den is inevitable in the world of man, a guaranteed outcome of man's choices. Daniel knows this because he understands God's plan. That is why he has peace right now, kneeling on this floor in front of these lions, because he feels the love of God's plan right now.

The garden was the plan, but man turned away and created a den instead. Man created a den that God cannot enter, but His love for us would not let that be the end. The Father decided He would take away the lions in our dens because His plan of love would not be stopped. That is what Daniel has cherished all of these years, and it has given him peace while waiting.

He looks around the den. A cave carved and transformed into a cage. Dark and dirty, and full of filth. Daniel can see the carcasses of the prisoners before him, bones illustrating hopelessness. The smell of feces burns his nostrils, embodying the defecation of faith man has brought. But in the midst of all of this contamination, Daniel can still feel their celestial presence.

"There is joy in the presence of God's angels,"[204] Daniel prays, "They are spirits sent from God to care for those who will receive salvation.[205] The Father orders His angels to protect me wherever I go, even into the den. For this I will praise the Lord now."[206]

Daniel entered his den with confidence. God has shown him everything and he rests in that. He kneels with reverence now in this holy place and asks to see one more thing. In his curiosity, he prays asking God to allow him to see them. He wants to see this sight, not in a dream, but with his own eyes.

"My Lord, I have been waiting for so many years. For so many years I have been on my knees with You. Praising, praying, and pleading. I have not always understood Your answers, but I have always trusted in

---

[204] Luke 15:10

[205] Hebrews 1:14

[206] Reference to Psalm 4:10.

them. I entered the den long before today... I have been persecuted, and I have had all praises given to me. I have had glory and riches, and I have felt the emptiness of poverty. Enemies and friendships have created my home. Health and sickness have guided my body. Wisdom and folly have guided my actions... All of these have created my den for many years. But faith... my faith is what has allowed me to survive my den all of my life."

Daniel continues to strain his eyes to see them.

"My Lord, I have been faithful to You. I know this moment is not about the den, but about the angels in the den with me now. Please allow me to see them."

The Spirit comes to Daniel and opens his eyes.

The light is too bright. There are too many to count. The angels are holding the lions like babies, embracing them like cherished pets. Daniel loses his breath to the amazement of this scene. He collapses; the awe is too great for him to hold his body up any longer. Tears fill his eyes and his body begins to shake. The years of service have not prepared Daniel for this moment. No dream has ever been this great. For the first time, Daniel fully understands God's love.

"My Lord, I have no words to express myself right now. I thought I understood You clearly, but now I see Your true glory. Now I see Your true love."

Daniel is sobbing. How could he have ever resented the waiting? How could he have ever feared the den? It is here that God sent the angels. Beautiful and holy, the angels stand as an army ready to protect God's child.

"Lord, how can You love me this much? Who am I for You to send this army to protect me in this den? This may not be the den of my creating, but I have influenced many other dens and am not without sin. I deserve to be reckoned with here, but instead you sent me angels. I should be in this den alone, but You love me more than that. I knew that I had to survive this den to find my way home, but I did not know that You would use it to show me Your love."

"Daniel, you are very precious to God, so listen carefully to what I have to say to you. Stand up, for I have been sent to you... Do not be afraid, Daniel. Since the first day you began to pray for understanding and to humble yourself before your God, your request has been heard in heaven. I have come in answer to your prayer."[207] Daniel looks at all of the angels, and with a supernatural force he has a new vision. His strength leaves him, his face grows deathly pale, and he feels weak. An angel comes to Daniel and touches him, bringing him to his knees.[208]

Daniel looks down to the ground, unable to say a word.[209] He finally gains the courage to say, "I am terrified by the vision I have seen, my lord, and I am very weak. In my vision, 'I saw the Man, dressed in linen clothing, with a belt of pure gold... His body looked like a dazzling gem. From His face came flashes like lightning, and His eyes were like flaming torches... and His voice was like the roaring of a vast multitude...'"[210]

Daniel looks to the angel.[211]

"How can someone like me, your servant, talk to you, my lord? My strength is gone, and I can hardly breathe."[212]

"Don't be afraid, for you are deeply loved by God. Be at peace; take heart and be strong."[213]

The Spirit comes, and Daniel feels the breath coming back to his lungs. He accepts his vision, and knows that God's plan will prevail.

"O Lord, You are a great and awesome God! You always fulfill Your promises of unfailing love to those who love You and keep Your

---

[207] Daniel 10:12 NLT

[208] Reference to Daniel 10:8-10.

[209] Reference to Daniel 10:15.

[210] Reference to Daniel 10:5-6. Many theologians believe Daniel was having a vision of Jesus, foreshadowing Rev. 1:13-15.

[211] The Bible states this angel was Michael.

[212] Daniel 10:16-17 NLT

[213] Reference to Daniel 10:19.

commands. But we have sinned and done wrong. We have rebelled against You and scorned Your commands and regulations.[214] We have built dens, but You have sent angels. Our dens will continue on, but so will Your angels until the day Your plan is finished. Thank You for loving us."

The Spirit takes command, and the angels and lions bow low. Man cannot open this den or any other—only the Spirit can. The Spirit convicts the king's heart and Daniel is released.[215] But Daniel does not want to leave the den; it is too beautiful.

The Spirit speaks, "Go home now; the wait is done. Go your way until the end. You will rest, and then at the end of the days, you will rise again to receive the inheritance set aside for you."[216]

Daniel turns to leave. The angels follow behind him because he is a child of God.

---

[214] Daniel 9:4-5 NLT
[215] Reference to Daniel 6:20-23.
[216] Daniel 12:13 NLT

LOVE'S MERCY

Then the word of the Lord came to Jonah a second time: "Go to the great city of Nineveh and proclaim to it the message I give you." Jonah obeyed the word of the Lord and went to Nineveh… Jonah began by going a day's journey into the city, proclaiming, "Forty more days and Nineveh will be overthrown." The Ninevites believed God. A fast was proclaimed, and all of them, from the greatest to the least, put on sackcloth. When Jonah's warning reached the king of Nineveh, he rose from his throne, took off his royal robes, covered himself with sackcloth and sat down in the dust. This is the proclamation he issued in Nineveh: "By the decree of the king and his nobles: Do not let people or animals, herds or flocks, taste anything; do not let them eat or drink. But let people and animals be covered with sackcloth. Let everyone call urgently on God. Let them give up their evil ways and their violence. Who knows? God may yet relent and with compassion turn from his fierce anger so that we will not perish." When God saw what they did and how they turned from their evil ways, he relented and did not bring on them the destruction he had threatened. But to Jonah this seemed very wrong, and he became angry. He prayed to the Lord, "Isn't this what I said, Lord, when I was still at home? That is what I tried to forestall by fleeing to Tarshish. I knew that you are a gracious and compassionate God, slow to anger and abounding in love, a God who relents from sending calamity. Now, Lord, take away my life, for it is better for me to die than to live." When the sun rose, God provided a scorching east wind, and the sun blazed on Jonah's head so that he grew faint. He wanted to die, and said, "It would be better for me to die than to live."

Jonah 3:1-10, 4:1-3, 4:8

Once you were not a people, but now you are God's people; once you had not received mercy, but now you have received mercy.

1 Peter 2:10

For we were all baptized by one Spirit so as to form one body—whether Jews or Gentiles, slave or free—and we were all given the one Spirit to drink.

1 Corinthians 12:13

Anyone who claims to be in the light but hates a brother or sister is still in the darkness. Anyone who loves their brother and sister lives in the light, and there is nothing in them to make them stumble. But anyone who hates a brother or sister is in the darkness and walks around in the darkness. They do not know where they are going, because the darkness has blinded them.

1 John 2:9-11

If anyone has material possessions and sees a brother or sister in need but has no pity on them, how can the love of God be in that person? Dear children, let us not love with words or speech but with actions and in truth. This is how we know that we belong to the truth and how we set our hearts at rest in his presence.

1 John 3:17-19

Jonah walks with anger and frustration. He has contempt for everything this city offers, and he wants to see it fall. It is the only reason he has come, and now God is offering redemption for the people? His heart fills with bitterness. Jonah argues with the Lord, feeling that he has to convince the Lord that his perspective is the correct one.

"Did I not say before I left home that You would do this, Lord? That is why I ran away to Tarshish! I knew that You are a gracious and compassionate God, slow to get angry and filled with unfailing love. I knew how easily You would cancel Your plans for destroying these people. Just kill me now, Lord! I'd rather be dead than alive because nothing I predicted is going to happen."[217]

With a bruised ego, Jonah walks to the east side of the city. There is a small alcove against a crumbling wall looking onto the city. He fashions a shelter there as he complains.[218]

"I have been faithful. You have chosen me to prophesy.[219] I know my relationship with You is chosen. And I have given my entire life to You. But You had me swallowed whole into darkness, and I still only praised You."[220]

There is no tree to provide shade for Jonah, and the spot is open to the consequences of constant sun. His determination to see vengeance against the city is greater than his discomfort from the sun. He will wait to see if anything happens. He needs something to happen to justify his heart.

"I lived in that fish for three days... like the faithful Isaac marching up the hill for three days... I, too, served You faithfully. I was not running from You, but from the filth of this world that lies in Nineveh. I wanted to stay pure and faithful in my worship of You, and not have the world corrupt me. But in that fish, I realized that I cannot be corrupted because my heart is true. I found favor with You, and You released me from my prison. So I came here to Nineveh, offering my wisdom to the people, and they rejected me."

Jonah's eyes focus harder on the town. He is cursing the sin that lives there.

---

[217] Jonah 4:2-3 NLT

[218] Jonah 4:5 NLT

[219] There were around fifty prophets in Israel from the time of Moses to Malachi. Jonah was chosen by God to be a prophet.

[220] This is a reference to Jonah being swallowed by a large fish in Jonah 1.

"Lord, how can I reach people like this? I came to this filthy city filled with contemptible people who do not deserve You. They cannot be who You save; You did not call them as Your chosen children. You cannot love them like You love me."

Jonah has not learned. His heart has not softened or humbled. The fish did nothing. Ego and pride still rule his heart. His faith is clouded by his prejudice. Neither in the black darkness of the fish or white blazing light of the sun does Jonah see the truth. There is no room left for God's work to be done.

The sun is high in the sky now, beating down on Jonah like a judge condemning the guilty. The heat takes his breath away, but he continues to wait. The Lord looks down upon Jonah with disappointment. Yet... the Father still loves His son... even though Jonah never questioned why. He was born into faith; it surrounded his childhood and Jonah has never known a time without it. But now his faith is numb, expected, and entitled. He has never asked the Father "why him" like so many prophets before. He was not surprised that the Father chose him. What Jonah does not understand is that the Father chose him despite his pride. The Father chose him because He knew Jonah needed to experience a miracle to end the pride.

So, like Nineveh, the Father will continue to show love to Jonah. The Lord arranges for a leafy plant to grow next to Jonah's alcove.[221] He makes it grow strong and high, with broad leaves to shade Jonah from the harsh sun.

Jonah knows God has blessed him with the shade and is grateful. Jonah feels God is justifying his heart's contempt. Jonah reasons that God must agree with him, and has given him comfort where he can watch punishment fall on the sinful people.

"My anger against these people is justified. The Lord agrees, and has provided me with shade."

The Lord speaks.

---

[221] Reference to Jonah 4:6.

"Is it right for you to be angry about this?"[222]

"Of course, these people do not honor Your law or holiness. They should be judged."

"Do not sin by letting anger gain control over you. Do not let the sun go down while you are still angry, for anger gives a mighty foothold to the Devil."[223]

Jonah ignores the Father's conviction and continues on with his prejudice. In His disappointment, God prepares a worm. The next morning, at dawn, the worm eats through the stem of the plant, and it quickly withers away, leaving Jonah exposed again to the sun. The sun grows hot, and God sends a scorching east wind to blow on Jonah. The sun beats on his head until he grows faint and wishes to die.[224] In his anger, Jonah yells at the Lord.

"Please, Lord, take me away from this sun. The depths of the ocean are better than this... Death is certainly better than this!"[225] The sun is strangling Jonah, and there is no air left in his lungs—just the heat and pressure from the sun. A pathetic plea crumbles out of his mouth as he gasps for air.

"Lord, kill me now because the sun is too great; it is judging me instead of the people of Nineveh. No justice is found in this cursed place."

God does not answer in anger. He has been patient with Jonah for a long time and will continue because He loves His son.

"Is it right for you to be angry because the plant died?"[226]

"Yes, even angry enough to die!"[227]

"You feel sorry about the plant, though you did nothing to put it there."[228]

---

[222] Jonah 4:4 NLT
[223] Ephesians 4:26–27 NLT
[224] Reference to Jonah 4:7–8.
[225] Jonah 4:8 NLT
[226] Jonah 4:9 NLT
[227] Jonah 4:9 NLT
[228] Jonah 4:10 NLT

Jonah is silent. He feels confused and betrayed.

"Do you know how to create a plant?"

Jonah is silent.

"Do you know what to put inside a seed for it to grow into a structure?"

Jonah is silent.

"Do you know how to mix the soil with the right nutrients it needs to thrive?"

Jonah is silent.

"Do you know how to turn a seed into a strong stalk?"

Jonah begins to feel humbled in his silence.

"Did you place each plant in this earth in its correct spot? Did you decide how long each would live?"

Jonah's heart begins to feel convicted.

"A plant is only, at best, short lived.[229] But my children will be with Me for eternity. I have created each one with love and care. I have decided their eye color, how their hair will grow, and where their footsteps will take them. I have not created many races, but only one race. The race of man. You have not been chosen to be My only salvation, but to set the example for salvation. Nineveh has more than 120,000 people living in spiritual darkness... should I not feel sorry for a great city?"[230]

Jonah covers his eyes from the sun so he can look at the city. He sees some children playing at the gates. He notices that they look very much like the ones in his village. How many children were in the city, Jonah wonders? God hears his thoughts.

"There are many."

Jonah sees men mending their nets in preparation to fish on the river.[231] He wonders how much they have to catch to feed their families? God answers his thoughts again.

---

[229] Reference to Jonah 4:10 NLT.

[230] Jonah 4:11 NLT

[231] Nineveh was located on the eastern bank of the Tigris River. Fishermen mended nets daily.

"Three full nets a day. One to feed their families and two to pay taxes. But the river has not provided for them in weeks."

Jonah imagines the fear that must come when you cannot provide for your family. Jonah squints again and sees the city differently. He sees a man at the gate; he looks like a decomposed corpse. God answers Jonah's thoughts once more.

"Disease and sickness have swept across the city like a thief."[232]

"I did not share much with them. I made it about the prophet and not the prophecy."

Jonah thought he knew the plan, but now he knows he never understood. He never even understood the Father. Jonah thought he was chosen, but now he knows God cannot choose a heart of hate to do His work. Jonah feels shame. Is Nineveh's filth darker than his own prideful heart?

"Jonah, your prejudice is focused on the wrong enemy. Do not look toward behaviors, people, or cities. The whole world is filled with filth, and it will never go away until each child knows Me. Cities will continue to fall, people will continue to hate, and the world will continue to crumble until My love fills each child's heart. Nothing can fix man's sins except for My plan of the Son. Turn your prejudice toward sin, and then you will win battles."

Jonah looks to the sun, and the Spirit comes, relieving the suffocating pressure from the heat, and filling Jonah's lungs with a new breath. He is not worthy of it, he knows.

"My son, I love you. I have done everything I can, even altered nature over and over again, to rescue you from your blindness. Yes, you serve Me faithfully, but you are not greater than the one who does not know Me. Jonah, you turn anyone who is different from you into an enemy. You have no enemies, because your sin is no different than theirs. All men and women are My children. I shed tears for all. My

---

[232] Around 765-759 BC the people of Nineveh suffered from several plagues that killed many.

desire is for all to know Me. I spared the sailors when they acted on faith and called out to Me. I spared the city when I saw that Nineveh put a stop to their evil ways; I had mercy on them and did not carry out the destruction I had threatened. The city's revival will show My glory for all time.[233] And now, I show you mercy. Mercy has always been my plan. No one is beyond redemption through My mercy. My mercy is for everyone; that is My great love."

---

[233] Theologians believe the revival at Nineveh was the greatest in history. The city's population was around 600,000. The Bible records that even the animals fasted for the Lord. Jews to this day still celebrate "The Day of Atonement," a holy day to honor what God did in Nineveh.

LOVE'S COMPLETION

When the Lord first spoke through Hosea, the Lord said to Hosea, "Go, take to yourself a wife of whoredom and have children of whoredom, for the land commits great whoredom by forsaking the Lord." So he went and took Gomer, the daughter of Diblaim, and she conceived and bore him a son. And the Lord said to him, "Call his name Jezreel, for in just a little while I will punish the house of Jehu for the blood of Jezreel, and I will put an end to the kingdom of the house of Israel. And on that day, I will break the bow of Israel in the Valley of Jezreel." She conceived again and bore a daughter. And the Lord said to him, "Call her name No Mercy, for I will no more have mercy on the house of Israel, to forgive them at all. But I will have mercy on the house of Judah, and I will save them by the Lord their God. I will not save them by bow or by sword or by war or by horses or by horsemen." When she had weaned No Mercy, she conceived and bore a son. And the Lord said, "Call his name Not My People, for you are not my people, and I am not your God.

Hosea 1:2-9

For I know the plans I have for you," declares the Lord, "plans to prosper you and not to harm you, plans to give you hope and a future.

Jeremiah 29:11

See what great love the Father has lavished on us, that we should be called children of God! And that is what we are! The reason the world does not know us is that it did not know him.

1 John 3:1

Above all, love each other deeply, because love covers over a multitude of sins.

1 Peter 4:8

Hosea looks across the table at Gomer once more. He questions if he can proceed, because it is all wrong. The proper customs have not been regarded. Hosea is trying to have faith, but he is confused. He did not set out to have this kind of life. He is fulfilled in serving only the Lord, and dedicating his entire life for His work. Why would God call him to do something different? To do something so shameful and condemning? What glory could this path bring?

Hosea begins to count all of the ways this is wrong. It is the wrong season. Autumn is the ideal time; harvest would be in, and minds would be at rest then.[234] There has been no betrothal period. How can they proceed to the marriage ceremony without the year-long betrothal?[235] A wedding like this is not done among his people. Who will come to a feast of this shameful union? Who will sing songs of rejoicing to the bride? Who will join in the procession? Who will be there to bless them? How can there be a consummation, when the bride has known so many others?[236] He has known no one, but has kept his body as a holy temple for the worship of the Lord. Now he is supposed to love one who has treated her body as a playground? In honesty, it turns his stomach. He must have it all wrong.

He looks to Gomer and tries to read her face. Does she want this union? Why is she agreeing to it? He turns from Gomer, falls to his

---

[234] Traditional Hebrew weddings were conducted after the harvest.

[235] Tradition required a couple to be engaged for a year before the wedding ceremony.

[236] Gomer was a known prostitute.

knees, and questions the Lord once more. Once more, the Lord is clear about Hosea's calling. He is not only supposed to marry her, but love her completely. Hosea remembers hearing God's voice clearly...

"Go and marry a girl who is a prostitute, so that some of her children will be born to you from other men. This will illustrate the way my people have been untrue to me, committing open adultery against me by worshipping other gods."[237]

"My God, how could I marry such a woman?"

"Go, marry her... and have children with her."

"Who will accept this union? Who would approve?"

"Whose approval do you need beyond My own? Whose command do you need beyond Mine?"

"My Lord, there is no one who has command over my heart and mind other than You. I will obey, but please tell me what glory this union will bring to Your name?"

"The glory will be the completion of My salvation..."

Gomer, the daughter of Diblaim, is now the wife of the prophet of Hosea. She is baffled herself. She lived in a world where idols come with a sensual touch, and pleasure was the only guiding rule. She delighted in the raisin cakes set at her table, and was ready to feast on them all of her days, no matter how often they left her hungry.[238]

When Hosea came to her, she thought he was like the other men who found her beauty desirable. She likes being desired by men—it gives her power and control. But Hosea did not desire her beauty; he came to her with a committed heart. He offered her love. She has heard many men use that word to serve their own purposes, but Hosea offered it freely, without expectations. She did not understand why he chose her, but it intrigued her. Her other relationships with men were empty, and Hosea promised her more. He had a plan with her at the center of it. He made her feel different, so she decided to try his plan.

---

[237] Hosea 1:2 TLB

[238] Gomer made sex and luxuries, like the delicacy of raisin cakes, her idols. Reference to Hosea 3:1.

Now she is at the chuppah second-guessing everything, with only her thoughts to counsel her.[239]

"I do not find him attractive—not his body, mind, or soul. He is boring and does not want to experience life..."

Gomer begins to feel the heat of the day.

"I have known men like him before; they are full of contradictions and hypocrisies, so why should I care about how he leads as a husband? Why should I care if it is the truth or not?"

Gomer laughs at Hosea under her breath; she finds him so awkward.

"He is so old; he is not in touch with my modern way of thinking; he will never understand me. He will oppress me."

Hosea's heart feels the conviction of the sacred altar, and he knows he has to obey, even without answers to his questions. He rises from his knees, takes Gomer by her hand, and makes her his wife. No betrothal, no ceremony, no procession, and no songs of praise. Just he and she quietly, with only the Lord to rejoice from it.

The days go by, and the plan is challenging for Gomer. She feels like it is nothing but rules to control her freedom. She wants to feel the excitement and power again from men, and live the kind of life that is for her enjoyment only. She tries Hosea's love, but it is too hard to understand, and it does not allow her to run free. She no longer wants Hosea's love; she will find something else more exciting. She convinces herself this is the truth.

The days have turned into years. The years have been long, and Hosea cannot follow the plan any longer. The continuous carousel of nights of waiting alone and days feeling forsaken, has left Hosea's heart full of doubt and pain. He gives over and over to Gomer, and over and over again she rejects his love. When she needs something, she comes back to him with the promise of change, but the change never comes, and she leaves again. Does she not understand that

---

[239] Chuppah is the Jewish altar or canopy used for weddings.

Hosea has provided everything for her? Does she not understand that it has been his love that has supported her? Does she not understand that only Hosea's love offers her truth and promise? No, she does not understand that, for she still runs off to her other lovers for false love.

Her rebellion and unfaithfulness advance. She decides enough is enough and rejects Hosea's plan completely. Children come, and the Lord names them to reveal the sin of the world.[240] Jezreel will sow God's destruction, Lo-Ruhamah will not be loved, and Lo-Ammi will never belong. Gomer does not mind what they represent, because their names reveal her own soul. She feels disgraced, not loved, and not of Hosea's people.[241] Gomer looks up to the sky and shouts out, "If Hosea's God is claiming this of my children, then that is fine, because I no longer want to be claimed by this God." She leaves.

Hosea questions how this marriage is part of the Lord's plan? It must all have been a mistake. Once again Hosea falls on his knees.

"Lord, I obeyed your commands and brought this woman into my home as my wife. Why would you choose this woman for me? Why do You want her as Your daughter? I have loved her faithfully. It was a love I gave freely and blindly, and she has abused it over and over again. I am the victim, the one abused and left to bandage my own cuts. Cuts that are too deep for repair. How can I welcome her back after the years of pain she has caused? How can I go on?"

The Father sees his torment and confusion.

"Father, I cannot love any longer. My strength is all gone."

"Do not grieve, for the joy of the Lord is your strength."[242]

"But, Lord, she has gone and turned her back on me."

---

[240] Reference to Hosea 1:4-5.

[241] Gomer had a son named Jezreel, of the disgraced city, meaning God sows. She then had a daughter named Lo-Ruhamah, meaning "not loved," and a second son named Lo-Ammi, meaning "not my people."

[242] Nehemiah 8:10

"All of us, like sheep, have strayed away. We have left God's paths to follow our own, yet the Lord laid on him the sins of us all.[243] It is the Thief... the Thief that comes only to steal and kill and destroy..."[244]

"Yes, the Thief has stolen her away and made her look to her other lovers instead of me. The Thief has taken her life and my marriage. The covenant is broken."

"Your marriage is not your covenant to claim, but Mine. Like Adam, Gomer broke My covenant and rebelled against Me, not you.[245] She is the daughter of this sinful world who chose to reject My plan. I created Adam to live with Me, and made a covenant with him to live forever in My presence, but he chose the unknown promise of death. My blessings cannot come without obedience. Obedience is not a punishment, but the only way to find Me. I give covenants as an act of grace; without them you have no way of reaching Me. Gomer, like all of My children, will never have enough obedience so My final covenant will come with forgiveness from the Son. You must have a forgiving heart too and love her. Love her as I love my children. Love her over and over again. My final covenant will bring them all back to Me. Adam may have fallen, but My plan has not. Adam was not the promise of the covenant, not Noah, not Abraham, not David. I have come that all may have life, and have it to the full.[246] Go and get your wife again. Bring her back to you and love her, even though she loves adultery.[247] If she does not come, try again... and again. Above all, love each other deeply, because love covers over a multitude of sins.[248] My love will cover all of your pain and bring forgiveness. Trust My love to heal this marriage."

---

[243] Isaiah 53:6 NLT
[244] John 10:10
[245] Reference to Hosea 6:7.
[246] John 10:10
[247] Hosea 3:1 NLT
[248] 1 Peter 4:8 NLT

The Spirit fills Hosea with His breath, giving him the strength to go on. Hosea picks himself up off his knees and goes in search of his wife. He thinks of God's plan and how his love for his wife is part of it. She is the world. A world that has done nothing but reject love over and over again. Rebellion against something unknown and misunderstood.

Hosea finds Gomer sold into the slavery of her sin.[249] In a prison of her own making, she no longer feels worthy. After years of abusing her body, the toll has caught up with her. Gomer has prostituted her soul for the Deceiver's lies. But Hosea has still come to bring her back. Hosea has still come to love her. Gomer does not understand and tries to send him away, too ashamed of herself to face him. Hosea whispers a prayer asking for strength, and the Spirit comes and fills him. He is ready to take on the price of her sin. What are pieces of silver and barley compared to gaining back his love?[250] He pays the ransom and redeems his wife.

Gomer does not understand and questions him.

"How can this be? Why do you welcome me with open arms? I have turned against you. I have not shown you love. I have not obeyed your covenant. Why do you pay the price of my sin? Why do you love me?"

Why? The little word that roars in the Father's ears. The children will never understand because they cannot understand His love. The Father tells Hosea to show Gomer His love now.

Hosea reaches out his hand to Gomer's.

"Your guilt has been justified. Your past has been forgotten. Your shame was left with the dust of yesterday. Be free of fear. There is no regret in my heart. Take my hand now and there will never be distance from my arms again."

---

[249] Reference to Hosea 3:2.

[250] Hosea has to pay fifteen pieces of silver and five bushels of barley to buy Gomer back.

Gomer takes his hand. All else has failed her; she will go with Hosea. She understands the justification and redemption, and she accepts the new covenant. A covenant of taking his hand and trusting. He is the Salvation, and she is the Completion.[251] Only Gomer can complete Hosea. Only His children can complete His plan... and only His plan can claim and recreate Jezreel—sowing God's love. Only His plan can call His children "my people... and the ones I love."[252]

---

[251] The name Gomer means completion.
[252] Reference to Hosea 1:11—God renames Gomer's children.

LOVE'S RENEWAL

The prophecy that Habakkuk the prophet received. How long, Lord, must I call for help, but you do not listen? Or cry out to you, "Violence!" but you do not save? Why do you make me look at injustice? Why do you tolerate wrongdoing? Destruction and violence are before me; there is strife, and conflict abounds. Therefore, the law is paralyzed, and justice never prevails. The wicked hem in the righteous, so that justice is perverted.

Habakkuk 1:1-4

Have I not commanded you? Be strong and courageous. Do not be afraid; do not be discouraged, for the Lord your God will be with you wherever you go.

Joshua 1:9

Peace I leave with you; my peace I give you. I do not give to you as the world gives. Do not let your hearts be troubled and do not be afraid.

John 14:27

I have told you these things, so that in me you may have peace. In this world you will have trouble. But take heart! I have overcome the world.

John 16:33

All Scripture is God-breathed and is useful for teaching, rebuking, correcting, and training in righteousness, so that the servant of God may be thoroughly equipped for every good work.

2 Timothy 3:16-17

He comes home dragging his feet. Another day and nothing has been accomplished. Habakkuk feels his spirit drained, and he questions what difference he is making in this crumbling world. Why did God choose him for this job? No one listens and no one cares. He is always going uphill without any view of the valley. Nothing grows at the top of this mountain. It is too cold; the land is dead and nothing prospers. Anger overtakes Habakkuk's heart, and he shouts out to God.

"How long, O Lord, must I call for help? But You do not listen! 'Violence!' I cry, but You do not come to save. Must I forever see this sin and misery all around me? Wherever I look, I see destruction and violence. I am surrounded by people who love to argue and fight. The law has become paralyzed and useless, and there is no justice given in the courts. The wicked far outnumber the righteous, and justice is perverted with bribes and trickery."[253]

God smiles. His days are so short. He encompasses all time—past, present, and future—with one blink of His eye. He empathizes with His children's worries, but holds too much in His hand to pause. God sees the glory of His finished plan. Everything else is just a story He is writing to accomplish it. He speaks to Habakkuk with joy in His heart.

"Look at the nations and be amazed! Watch and be astounded at what I will do! For I am doing something in your own day, something you would not believe even if someone told you about it."[254]

God will use everything: enemies, war, sickness, death, peace, and love to accomplish His plan. His children are not forgotten—He is in control and understands the script He is writing. But Habakkuk does

---

[253] Habakkuk 1:1-3 NLT
[254] Habakkuk 1:5 NLT

not trust that God fully understands the pain and suffering. He feels he has to complain more so the Lord can grasp how much is wrong. He challenges the Lord one more time.

"O Lord my God, my Holy One, You who are eternal—is Your plan in all of this to wipe us out? Surely not! O Lord our Rock, You have decreed the rise of these Babylonians to punish and correct us for our terrible sins. You are perfectly just in this. But will You, who cannot allow sin in any form, stand idly by while they swallow us up? Should You be silent while the wicked destroy people who are more righteous than they? Are we but fish to be caught and killed? Are we but creeping things that have no leader to defend them from their enemies? Must we be strung up on their hooks and dragged out in their nets while they rejoice? Then they will worship their nets and burn incense in front of them. 'These nets are the gods who have made us rich!' they will claim. Will you let them get away with this forever? Will they succeed forever in their heartless conquests?"[255]

Again, the Father smiles down on His child. Spoiled and impatient, Habakkuk wants everything in his own time. What Habakkuk does not understand is that God's time is far better. His time knows no boundaries and limits. His time knows only prosperity and glory.

"Things I plan will not happen right away. Slowly, steadily, surely, the time approaches when the vision will be fulfilled. If it seems slow, wait patiently, for it will surely take place. It will not be delayed."[256]

"Father, I have been preaching for twenty-three years and I am still waiting.[257] Waiting for my words to matter in a world where evil triumphs."

Habakkuk feels pride in his challenge and remonstrates more.

"Father, it has been thousands of years and we are all still waiting for You. Waiting for You to bring goodness and peace. How cunning

---

[255] Habakkuk 1:12-17 NLT
[256] Reference to Habakkuk 2:3.
[257] Theologians believe Habakkuk's ministry lasted from 612-589 BC.

the serpent was to bring choice into the world. Why do You allow it to continue? Why do You not end all of this evil? The darkness of the evil is extinguishing the light of life. Why does the darkness shine brighter than the light?"

"Am I not the God who created the world with just My breath? Am I not the God who wanted more, so I made My children from the dust of My feet? Am I not the God who saved My son Adam from death? Am I not the God who provided an ark of salvation for Noah? Am I not the God who created an Exodus for My children? Am I not the God of an eternal covenant for those who love Me? I love this world far more than you ever could. It is My heart that breaks when My ears hear their screams. It is My tears that cover this earth when their pain is too much. It is My love that warms their cold nights. And yet, it is My name they curse. It is My plan they reject. It is My salvation they deny. Darkness will always continue to grow as long as the children reject me. No speech, no assembly, no government, no minister... no plan will ever bring the light without Me."

God once again smiles, fills Habakkuk with His Spirit, and whispers into his ear.

"Come close... hear My words now... this is still My creation, and I make no mistakes. Wait and trust; then you will see amazing things. I will give all of My authority in heaven and earth to Him."[258]

Habakkuk breathes in the Spirit and listens.

"For a child will be born, a Son given to you. The government will rest on His shoulders. These will be His royal duties: Wonderful Counselor, Mighty God, Everlasting Father, and Prince of Peace.[259] For I have chosen Him before creation of the world. In Him the plan will prevail. He will bring unity to all things in heaven and earth. In Him, everything will work out with the purpose of My plan. When the world believes, the children will be marked by Him with a seal and the promise of the

---

[258] Reference to Matthew 28:18.
[259] Isaiah 9:6 NLT

Holy Spirit, guaranteeing their inheritance of My glory. He will be seated with Me, and rule over all authority, power, and dominion for now and in all ages to come. I will place all things under His feet, and appoint Him to be head over everything for the church.[260] The Lord is in His holy temple. Let all the earth be silent before Him."[261]

Habakkuk trembles inside, and his lips quiver in fear when he hears all this. His legs give way from beneath him.[262] He feels the awe of God's great power and he knows there are no more reasons to worry. God will provide for this world.

"I will wait quietly for the coming day when disaster will strike the people who invade us. Even though the fig trees have no blossoms, and there are no grapes on the vine; even though the olive crop fails, and the fields lie empty and barren; even though the flocks die in the fields, and the cattle barns are empty, yet I will rejoice in the Lord! I will be joyful in the God of my salvation. The sovereign Lord is my strength! He will make me as surefooted as a deer, and bring me safely over the mountains."[263]

The pastor feels renewed. The Father has seen his exhausted heart, and given him the direction he needs. Habakkuk opens the door and goes back out to the world to work.

---

[260] Reference to Ephesians 1:4-23.
[261] Habakkuk 2:20 NLT
[262] Reference to Habakkuk 3:16.
[263] Habakkuk 3:16-19 NLT

LOVE'S STILLNESS

Malachi written 430 BC – James written AD 49[264]

Before the mountains were born or you brought forth the whole world, from everlasting to everlasting you are God... A thousand years in your sight are like a day that has just gone by, or like a watch in the night.

Psalm 90:2-4

For everything there is a season, and a time for every matter under heaven: a time to be born, and a time to die; a time to plant, and a time to pluck up what is planted; a time to kill, and a time to heal; a time to break down, and a time to build up; a time to weep, and a time to laugh; a time to mourn, and a time to dance; a time to cast away stones, and a time to gather stones together; a time to embrace, and a time to refrain from embracing... He has made everything beautiful in its time. Also, he has put eternity into man's heart, but even so, people cannot see the whole scope of God's work from beginning to end.

Ecclesiastes 3:1-5, 11 NLT

---

[264] There were approximately four hundred years between the Old Testament book of Malachi and the New Testament book of Matthew. This period is often referred to as the "Four Hundred Silent Years." Matthew is the first book of the New Testament, but chronologically, James is the first book.

He said to them, "It is not for you to know times or seasons that the Father has fixed by his own authority.

Acts 1:7

He made known to us the mystery of his will according to his good pleasure, which he purposed in Christ... to be put into effect when the times reach their fulfillment—to bring unity to all things in heaven and on earth under Christ.

Ephesians 1:9-10

Yet you do not know what tomorrow will bring. What is your life? For you are a mist that appears for a little time and then vanishes.

James 4:14

But do not overlook this one fact, beloved, that with the Lord one day is as a thousand years, and a thousand years as one day. The Lord is not slow to fulfill his promise as some count slowness, but is patient toward you, not wishing that any should perish, but that all should reach repentance.

2 Peter 3:8-9 NKJ

Yahweh speaks through Malachi... "I will send My messenger, who will prepare the way before Me. Then suddenly the Lord you are seeking will come to His temple; the Messenger of the covenant, whom you desire, will come."[265]

Yahweh speaks again, "But who can endure the day of His coming? Who can stand when He appears? For He will be like a refiner's fire or a launderer's soap. He will sit as a refiner and purifier of silver; He will purify the Levites and refine them like gold and silver. Then once more the Lord will accept the offerings brought to Him by the people... I am the Lord, and I do not change. That is why you descendants of Jacob are not already completely destroyed. Ever since the days of your ancestors,

---

[265] Malachi 3:1

you have scorned My laws and failed to obey them. Now return to Me, and I will return to you."[266]

Malachi's work is finished. It is time for quiet. The Spirit and Son kneel at the Father's feet, and the Father speaks.

"Malachi will be the last author for right now."[267]

"The children will believe You are silent, and they will become angry." The Spirit is emphatic.

"They misunderstand silence as indifference," the Son agrees. "For thousands of years they used it as an excuse in the beginning."[268] The Son pauses and looks down at Malachi. "The children do not understand the divine gift You have given them... a unified story of prophets and law to prepare a way for the Word to come in the flesh... they will forget and only listen to the silence."

The Spirit looks to the Father. "Every time We are quiet, they turn; over and over again it has happened."

The Son looks to the Father as well. "They will cry out in pain, saying that Your silence is deafening."

The Father smiles. "I know. They want an author for every moment.[269] They want to hear with their ears, rather than listen with their hearts. They have redesigned time to fit into their boundaries—worshipping it, thinking it can protect, encourage, and determine their lives. My children do not understand that I created time to glorify only Me; it's not their own to shape or to manage. The hours, the days, the weeks, the years are all Mine."

"They will say You are abusing time," the Son adds.

The Father smiles and looks across His creation. He gave the sun and moon as a gift to His children to help them remember moments, but not to define them. Time is flexible and cannot be held; like water

---

[266] Malachi 3:2-7

[267] The book of Malachi is the last book of the Old Testament.

[268] Reference to the time between Adam and Noah recorded in the Bible.

[269] Reference to the prophets who led the people and wrote the Old Testament.

in the hand, it cannot be contained. It flows and escapes without law or relativity. His children have turned time into an idol. From the moment they open their eyes they are counting the minutes, filling the minutes, and planning the minutes instead of lifting their eyes to Him. The children look to time to heal, look to time to prepare, and look to time to lead the way instead of looking to Him. The children want to control what happens and when; they become angry when time is not what they planned. They carry the disappointment of time with them in their hearts—heavy and filled with despair instead of the faith of His promises.

The children have created a timeline marking the Father's quietness as silence over and over again. Focusing on the gaps as moments of disregard and lack of love, the children do not understand that the gaps are filled with the Father's love. There is no love in silence, but in quietness the children can feel the Father's love fully. Silence is the absence of sound. Silence is the prohibition of speaking, whether speaking in joy or sorrow. The Father has never had an absence of anything; His quietness is not silence. The Father's quietness is carried out discreetly with moderation, but never with the lack of regard or love. The Father's quietness shows His great patience with His children. He has the capacity to accept and tolerate their rejection without getting angry or disowning the children. Instead, the Father waits patiently in quietness, allowing them to cry, mourn, and rejoice the way they need to fill the timeline. Always waiting for them to turn back to Him.

He looks across His creation and smiles, for He knows that He *is* time.

"My Son, this will be just a moment. Adam was just a few days ago.[270] They are not ready yet for You to enter. We have to be quiet to give them the time to need Us, to come to Us, and to choose Us. It has always been their choice on how long it takes. What is four hundred

---

[270] Reference to 2 Peter 3:8–9. Thousands of years are like days to God.

years to prepare the way for You? What were thousands of years to prepare for Noah? Where was the author for Abraham? Who encouraged Moses? There was never silence for them—I was always there guiding and loving. We will be in this four-hundred-year pause actively, like We have always been. Some will see and feel Us, but many will not. They will only understand time. They will mistake quietness for silence. They will not understand how it fits into My plan. My pauses only move the plan forward."

The Spirit breathes out onto creation, "The children only want Us to fill their hearts with power and answered prayers, winning their trust, making their faith strong and overflowing. They do not understand the seasons where chaos and darkness seem to carelessly shatter their lives. Their souls are crushed and they cry out, saying they need rescue. They want time to stop and for Us to yell louder than the chaos... but that is the season for quietness. The children allow their perception of Our quietness to become their reality. They do not know how We are conducting the entire world to move in time for Us to fill their lungs with breath. They do not know that quietness is the only way to prepare them for the next step. It is only in the quietness that they can learn to trust Our promises more than their perception."

"Father," the Son stands before Him, "I know that whatever You do is final. Nothing can be added to it or taken from it. Your purpose is that people should stand in awe of You. Whatever exists today and whatever will exist in the future has already existed in the past. For You call the past to account."[271] The Son looks back to the children. "Father, prepare me. Use this quietness to prepare me to serve them so I can bring balance to time and take away their silence forever."

The plan is not silenced; it moves forward.

---

[271] Ecclesiastes 3:14–15 NLT

LOVE'S CRADLE

And she gave birth to her firstborn, a son. She wrapped him in cloths and placed him in a manger, because there was no guest room available for them.

Luke 2:7

The scepter will not depart from Judah, nor the ruler's staff from between his feet, until he to whom it belongs shall come and the obedience of the nations shall be his.

Genesis 49:10

I see him, but not now; I behold him, but not near; a star will come out of Jacob; a scepter will rise out of Israel. He will crush the foreheads of Moab, the skulls of all the people of Sheth.

Numbers 24:17

But you, Bethlehem Ephrathah, though you are small among the clans of Judah, out of you will come for me one who will be ruler over Israel whose origins are from of old, from ancient times.

Micah 5:2

The farmer needs it quickly. He does not give it much thought or care; he just knows it has to be simple and work. He gathers the mud and straw together and begins to mold.[272] It does not need to be a great masterpiece or a work of art, he tells himself; it just needs to be able to hold scraps of food. The farmer's hands begin to ache from all the work, but eventually the mud and straw become cold and hard. It becomes a manger. It will sit to the side with no glory. It will often be overlooked. It will hold the spoils of the crops, serving its only purpose—to feed the animals.

The farmer moves the manger to its lowly place in the stable, and while he is filling it with hay, he is startled by a scream. The scream of a girl pierces the silence of the dark night, and it chills him to the bone. He comes to the opening of the stable and sees a young man carrying a girl who is obviously with child. The man catches the farmer's eye and comes running toward him. The man has panic in his voice and pleads for a bed for his wife. They both have a look of fear and desperation, and the farmer knows he has to help them. The farmer is about to offer his home to the poor couple, when something comes upon his spirit and stops him. Before he can think, he feels the words come out of his mouth.

"Use my stable; you can shelter here."

The man wastes no time and quickly rushes by the farmer to take his wife into the stable. The farmer does not understand what overcame him. He has room in his home, and he could tell the poor girl needed a bed. It is only customary to offer your home, so why did he not offer his home?[273] The young man seems so scared and unsure; how could he have turned him away? The farmer does not understand this spirit in him keeping him at a distance, but he stays away. The farmer runs inside, and looks at the scene from the solitude of his home.

---

[272] Mangers were often made of straw, mud, and rock.

[273] Hospitality was highly regarded in the Jewish culture. It was a common act to offer food or shelter to strangers.

His questions are not calmed by the girl's screams. Out in the night, she screams for hours. He understands the pains of childbirth can go on for a long time, and dreads that her screams will be his lullaby tonight. He wonders if he should go out there and offer help. Or should he go find a midwife? Every time he decides to act and reach for the door, something forces him to stay. As much as his heart feels convicted, he cannot bring himself to leave. Something is keeping him inside. It is not fear or lack of concern, but a feeling he cannot name. Every time he hears the girl cry out in pain, he feels a warm peace like a blanket come upon him. It is a peace he has never experienced before, nor does he understand where it is coming from. He knows he is not supposed to be there; something sacred is happening, he can feel it. His presence would be trespassing on holy ground.

Then the screams stop. The lullaby of the girl's cries end, and his spirit feels confused. What has happened? What is next? What should he do now? All of these thoughts rush through his mind, when suddenly he sees a light shining through the crack in his door. Cautious of his own curiosity, he slowly opens the door, only to shut it again quickly. An incredible bright light blinds him. He tries once again to look out, but he cannot see. He falls to his knees and listens. He cannot hear the girl or the man; all he hears is silence. He is straining his ears to catch any noise, when suddenly he hears the cries of a baby. Instantly, there is glorious singing from voices that are not human. The singing drowns out the cries of the baby. It is music like he has never heard before, and it brings tears to his eyes. He turns his eyes slowly upward and looks out the window to see the sky filled with beings that shine like the sun. Too many to count—more than all of the stars. He looks toward his stable, and there resting above it is a star of such beauty it takes his breath away. The farmer does not understand what is happening, but he knows his life is forever changed.

He sees shepherds approaching... shepherds leaving their flocks to come to his stable. What is happening, he questions? Shepherds do not leave their sheep. What glory is so great that would command that? He looks closer and notices all of the animals in his stable lying down. The animals almost look like they are in worship. Now the farmer notices the shepherds fall to their knees in worship as well. He is struggling to see what they are all bowing down to. Is the young man a great person? Is the girl someone of consequence? Could it be the child? Could it be possible they are bowing to a baby?

The farmer needs to understand. The Spirit that is keeping him inside is now pulling him toward the stable. The Spirit fills him with an eager breath, and the farmer knows he will not be fulfilled until he sees for himself. He moves to the door, opens it, and slowly approaches. The farmer realizes that he is crawling along the ground—something is keeping him from rising. It is not the beings in the sky or the blinding light. No, the farmer feels like his feet are not good enough to touch the ground.

He is too scared to get too close, so he stays behind all of the shepherds. The farmer slowly rises to his knees and he sees what is happening. There in his stable lies a baby in his manger. The light is cascading down upon Him, and the farmer knows. He does not understand how he knows, but he does. He knows what this nativity scene is. Tears fill his eyes.

Time passes, but it is all a blur to the farmer—he does not know if he has been on his knees for hours or days. He has seen so much; he can hardly take it all in. The star never goes away, even when the morning light comes. The angels' singing is still ringing in the farmer's ears. The shepherds have stayed; even the animals are still keeping watch over the baby. The baby is quiet now, the girl is at peace sleeping, and the man is watching over them. The farmer looks at the man and sees he is still carrying a burden. The farmer feels the man's burden is different from a typical father's need to provide for his family. The man's burden seems like he is carrying the world on his shoulders. The farmer looks closer and sees the man is crying. Slow, steady tears are raining down his cheeks, and he seems to be mumbling something in whispers. The farmer slowly creeps closer to hear what is escaping from his lips.

"Yahweh..."

The man chokes back a sob in his efforts not to wake the girl and baby. "Yahweh... please help me... I did not think I would love Him..."

The farmer does not understand this young father's confession, and imposes more on the prayer.

"I did not think of myself as His father—just Your servant doing the task you asked of me. You asked, and I was just obeying. But I see Him now, and He is my son... I love Him. I do not feel like your servant, just His father. How am I supposed to be His father and raise Him for the world? I do not want to give Him to the world... I want Him. She does not realize what you are asking, but I see it all clearly. This burden is too great for me; I understand Your plan. I cannot raise Him just to let Him go."

The farmer can see the tears escape the man's eyes. The sound is heavy, matching the burden resting on this man's shoulders. The farmer watches the man cry with his mind racing. There is so much glory in this moment, yet so much sadness. The farmer knows he is witnessing a father preparing for a son to leave him.

The man's tears eventually calm, and exhaustion overwhelms his body. The man lies with his family and falls asleep holding them. The farmer watches them—he cannot turn away. As sleep begins to weigh on his eyes, the farmer sees the man jump up, as if startled from a dream.[274] The man urgently wakes his wife and baby and takes them away. All becomes quiet again. The star fades away, the shepherds leave, the farmer can no longer see the angels, and the silence is deafening. The farmer is mourning the loss of it all ending. He enters his stable and walks to his manger. The object he gave no thought to became the cradle for the King. The farmer kneels down to look closer at his humble manger. He was so careless in creating it. He wished he had taken more time and used rock or wood. Made it bigger or grander. He thought it was just going to be a simple feeding trough, nothing more.

---

[274] Reference to Matthew 2:13-14.

He looks up and asks why. This place is not fit for the Messiah. Should not the Son of God come into this world with majesty and pomp like other kings? Should not great royalty come to pay their respects, rather than lowly shepherds who are cast off by society? Should not the place of his birth be sacred, rather than a place barely fit for animals?

The farmer looks down at his manger that once had no glory, and now it is the precious throne of God. He was wrapped in rags and lay against this dirty, coarse, misshapen manger, but then the heavens exploded with praise. Angels came in triumphantly with glory to proclaim the good news that the Son of God was lying in a manger. They claimed this was all to God's glory in the very highest. Glory to God the Savior in a feeding trough. Glory to God, the Messiah is here, and He lies in a mud trough only fit for animals. Glory to God. The only witnesses to this spectacular event are animals and lowly shepherds. The angels had proclaimed all of this was good news?

"I bring good news of great joy for everyone... Glory to God in the highest heaven..."[275]

The angels' praises linger in his mind. He can still hear them singing. The farmer is trying to reason why this place?—dark and cold, barely a cave. Why was this God's ordained place? This stable, this manger is the only way God's glory could be achieved? Not in his house or an inn? Not in a palace or among the elite? No, none of those were holy enough; it had to be a stable, it had to be a manger.

The thought about his stable and manger keeps going through the farmer's mind. His home is not holy enough for this event. Who is he to witness the birth of the Messiah? He is not an educated man, but he knew a little of the Scriptures. The farmer knew of Noah. God told Noah to build a ta-va.[276] It was a mighty and enormous fortress to save humanity from judgment. An ark to rescue man from

---

[275] Luke 2:10, 14

[276] Ta-va means "ark."

being washed away by sin. Then he thought about Moses. He, too, was placed in a ta-va, tiny but still mighty.[277] A basket of deliverance for His children. Now a tiny manger is used to bring salvation for His children. A small cradle made of mud and straw to save all humanity from now to all generations.

The farmer looks around and sees his humble stable with new eyes. He sees a holy palace fit for the one true King. The farmer knows this is the place He was supposed to be born. He is not an earthly king, but a heavenly one. What are the riches of the world to God? The King of kings does not need the comfort of the world; those comforts are not God's luxuries. This King decided to be born among the people He is here to save. The Son of Man came not to receive glory like earthly kings, but to give glory in a way no earthly king could ever do. This baby needed a mighty ta-va to enter the world to prepare Him for the way He will leave it.

The farmer takes God's gift of the cradle into his arms and thanks Him.

"El Roi..."[278]

The farmer is overcome with emotions.

"El Roi...You do truly see me. I do not know why You included me in Your plan, but thank You for this gift. This cradle is not supposed to hold the Son; You made this cradle to hold me. This cradle holds the light. This cradle holds the hope. This cradle holds the salvation. This cradle holds the love. Thank You for cradling me."

---

[277] The word for the basket Moses was placed in was ta-va. Ta-va is only used twice in the Bible, with Noah and Moses.

[278] El Roi means "God Who Sees Me."

LOVE'S CHOSEN

This is how the birth of Jesus the Messiah came about. His mother Mary was pledged to be married to Joseph, but before they came together, she was found to be pregnant through the Holy Spirit. Because Joseph her husband was faithful to the law, and yet did not want to expose her to public disgrace, he had in mind to divorce her quietly. But after he had considered this, an angel of the Lord appeared to him in a dream and said, "Joseph, son of David, do not be afraid to take Mary home as your wife, because what is conceived in her is from the Holy Spirit. She will give birth to a son, and you are to give him the name Jesus, because he will save his people from their sins" ...When Joseph woke up, he did what the angel of the Lord had commanded him and took Mary home as his wife... And he gave him the name Jesus.

Matthew 1:18-21, 24-25

Jesus's parents went to Jerusalem for the Festival of the Passover. When he was twelve years old, they went up to the festival, according to the custom. After the festival was over, while his parents were returning home, the boy Jesus stayed behind in Jerusalem, but they were unaware of it. Thinking he was in their company, they traveled on for a day. Then they began looking for him among their relatives and friends. When they did not find him, they went back to Jerusalem to look for him. After three days they found him in the temple courts, sitting among the teachers, listening to them, and asking them ques-

tions... When his parents saw him, they were astonished.
His mother said to him, "Son, why have you treated us like this? Your father
and I have been anxiously searching for you." "Why were you searching for
me?" he asked. "Didn't you know I had to be in my Father's house?"
But they did not understand what he was saying to them.

Luke 2:41-46, 48-50

So do not fear, for I am with you; do not be dismayed, for I am your God.
I will strengthen you and help you; I will uphold you with
my righteous right hand.

Isaiah 41:10

So you have sorrow now, but I will see you again; then you will rejoice,
and no one can rob you of that joy.

John 16:22 NLT

Joseph looks at her swollen belly, and wonders if the Father questions His choice in him. He does not understand fully what the future holds, but he understands that he is not able to do what Yahweh is asking of him. Joseph does not know how to be a father. He has been praying silently in his heart for months that the Father would take this all away, but instead her belly continues to grow larger and larger. Joseph knows the baby is coming soon and he is full of fear.

Joseph is cold and weary. He has walked miles and miles. Does the Father look down upon him now and feel disappointment? Does He wish He had chosen someone wiser? Why did the Father choose him? The night is getting darker, and Joseph feels the darkness all around him.

Joseph looks at Mary and feels responsible. How is he ever supposed to take care of the Mother of God? Will he ever be worthy? Does she know that he has loved her all along? He did not say yes out of duty, but out of love for her. He is questioning everything. Joseph feels so alone at this moment. Mary feels like a stranger, and he has been looking for his Father for days and has not found Him. Joseph's feet begin to ache.

They have been traveling for days. Long days. She needs a bed, and Joseph feels guilty that he has not been able to provide one for her. Every time Joseph hears her groan in pain, his fears grow larger, like her belly. Joseph fears everything, and his head is drowning in questions. The physical pain; will there be dangers with the labor? How can he help her through it? If the baby is God, then how does he hold Him? Will he hurt Him if he does not do it right? Will he be capable of loving Him like a true father? Is he worthy to love Him? Can he teach Him anything? Will he ever be able to pass on fatherly wisdom? What is his role in His life? Too many questions; his head hurts. Joseph's feet bleed.

Joseph has offered all he is to the Lord, and now the Father leaves him in silence. He feels so weak and has been begging the Lord for strength. *Why did He choose him? The Lord must have made a mistake,* Joseph tells himself. Joseph's thoughts are interrupted when Mary gasps and grabs her stomach. Panic sets in, but he must go on. They have been going on for miles, and Joseph knows he has to go on for as long as the Lord commands. This journey is just beginning for him. Joseph prays that God will give him the strength he needs to walk it.

Hours pass and he can see the pressure is getting greater for Mary now. The Son is coming tonight; he feels it. Joseph looks up, desperate. The night is so quiet and still, but the screams inside of his head are pounding like thunder. Suddenly, he sees water coming from her and without thinking he scoops her into his arms. Joseph tells himself to keep his voice calm. He has to be Mary's strength right now. He will find a place for them; he will not fail her in this. Joseph can tell her pain is intense, and she needs a bed. He focuses on keeping his arms strong, and ignores his trembling legs. Joseph carries her from door to door. With every door slam, he screams inside to God to help them. Finally, God provides a place.

The only option is disgusting: damp, moldy, and scratchy hay. Joseph complains in his heart to the Father for not providing a better place as he lays Mary down. He gasps at the foul odors of the animal's filth that fill his nostrils, and feels the spew coming up but swallows it back down. He must remain strong for Mary. Joseph refuses to be anything but a source of strength for Mary. She gets sick, and vomit is everywhere. Without hesitating, he quickly cleans her up. Tears begin to roll down Mary's cheeks and that breaks his heart. Joseph wants to take away all of her fears and pain.

None of this feels right. How can this be a part of the Father's plan? It's just a stable; barely fit for animals, how can this be the Lord's plan for His Son? Joseph feels so confused and helpless. Mary looks to Joseph, but he does not know how to help her. She seems so calm. Does she not doubt God's plan? Does she not feel like a stable is no place for the King to enter this world? Did God tell Mary something different? Does she have more faith? Is he lacking faith? All he feels right now is fear. The fear is taking all of his strength away—strength that he needs for her. Joseph has to use his faith. Finally, he stops screaming inside and whispers, "Father."

All seems to stop around him and there is stillness. He feels the Spirit come, like He did that first night.[279]

"Son."

"Yahweh, please..."

"I know, you do not have to ask. I am here; I have always been here."

"I have not felt You."

"Because you are only choosing to feel your fear, and I do not dwell in fear. Finally, you broke away from it to call to Me."

"I cannot do this. Why did You choose me? I do not know how to do what You are asking of me."

"Be still, and know I am Lord. Just breathe."

"I do not know how to breathe right now. I cannot feel any breath in my lungs."

---

[279] Reference to Matthew 1:20.

"Be still, My Spirit is your breath."

"She needs a clean place... a bed... someone to help her to do this..."

"All you need is Me."

"This is not a righteous place for His birth... He needs a holy place..."

"I am here; this is a holy place. No other place will do."

"But..."

"Son, stop arguing with me. My ways are perfect, this place is perfect, and My Son is perfect. Be still, and allow Me to enter into your heart so I can accomplish My plan."

Joseph becomes still and quiet, and the Holy Spirit comes upon him. He looks around and sees the stable differently; it is sacred ground now. Everything becomes holy. Mary looks up to him, and at last he sees love in her eyes. Joseph still does not understand why the Father chose him, but he knows in that moment that God will never leave him. Joseph knows God will help him on this journey no matter where it leads them. His role is to be her husband and Jesus's father, and he is going to do that faithfully. He looks down upon her bare stomach and legs and feels power. The fear is gone; he is ready to be a father. Joseph braces his body behind her for support, and wraps his arms around her as she takes a deep breath and pushes...

... The pushing... the pushing of crowds is overwhelming them. Joseph puts his body behind Mary for support, and wraps his arms around her. The crowds from the Passover festival are pushing them off the road.[280] Joseph's son may be twelve now, but he can still feel the baby he held in his arms for the first time in the stable.[281] Now they have been looking for Jesus for days; the Son is missing. Joseph sees the panic in Mary's eyes, and he tries to reassure her, but he feels the panic too. Joseph has failed her, and he has failed his son. Joseph is supposed to protect his son, and instead he leaves Him behind. Every moment

---

[280] Reference to Luke 2:41.

[281] Scholars believe Jesus was twelve years old when Joseph took Him to Jerusalem for Passover.

they do not find Jesus is crushing his heart more and more. How will they ever find Jesus through these crowds?

Why did the Lord choose him? Obviously, Joseph is not capable of this job. He has been praying silently in his heart for days that the Father will take this all away and bring his baby home to him. But instead, the crowds grow larger and larger, and Jesus seems farther and farther away from them. Joseph has known from the beginning that he does not understand what is coming in the future, but he has always trusted God to provide the path for him to walk. He tells himself now that God will bring their baby back to them. Joseph gently tells that to Mary to assure her. Joseph promises her he will never fail them again. Joseph promises God.

The crowds are thick now, and Joseph is having trouble seeing over the sea of strange faces. Does the Father look down upon him and feel disappointment? Does He wish He had chosen someone wiser? *Why did He not choose someone wiser,* Joseph questions. Fear is creeping in again. He tries to fight against it, but he questions everything. Is his little boy safe? Is He in pain? Jesus is God, but Joseph's little boy too. Is Joseph wrong if he fights for Him? His servant's heart is telling him to trust in God, but his father's love is saying to fight. He has spent years teaching Jesus all that he knows. Many times he has been embarrassed to do so, for who is he to teach God? But there were so many moments when Joseph forgot and only saw his little boy. A little boy who let Joseph hold Him, and looked to Joseph with admiration in His eyes—who looked up to Joseph like a real father. Joseph has questioned his role in Jesus's life many times, but every time he began, he would stop because he heard his son cry out "Daddy," and then he knew. He knew he was created to be Jesus's father fully and completely.

The crowds are never-ending. Joseph offers all he is to the Lord, and still the Father leaves him in silence. He feels so weak and begs the Lord for strength. Why did He choose him? Joseph feels pressure around his heart. It is tight and he loses his breath, but they must go on. They have been looking throughout Jerusalem for days.[282] Joseph knows the journey will not end when they find Jesus, because Joseph's purpose on this journey is changing. He understands that the last twelve years have been preparing his little boy to fulfill the Lord's will, and now it is time. This trip has taught Joseph that he cannot walk this path with his little boy any longer. He looks down to Mary; she does not understand this yet, and he knows she never will.

Hours pass and the pressure around Joseph's heart is getting greater. He has to find Jesus tonight. He looks up, desperate. They come to the courtyard of the temple.[283] Joseph feels the Spirit pulling him there. He hears the panic in Mary's voice; he has to be strong for her. He guides her through the crowds again. The crowds begin to part, and Joseph stops in his tracks. He tries to gasp for air, but the air never comes. Joseph sees the Son. Mary yells and runs to her baby. They both run to Him, and Mary engulfs Him in her arms.

"Son, why have you treated us like this? Your father and I have been anxiously searching for You."[284]

Jesus allows her to cradle Him, but He looks up to His Joseph. Joseph understands that he has forever lost his little boy, and tears escape from his eyes. Jesus sees the pain in His father's eyes. He breaks away from His mother gently, and holds her hands.

"Why were you searching for me?" He asks. "Didn't you know I had to be in My Father's house?"[285]

Mary looks at Him searchingly, but she cannot understand His meaning. Joseph understands. It is time for him to let his little boy go. Why did He choose him? Joseph is not capable of this. He looks away— he does not want Mary to see his tears. It all happened so fast. It was just yesterday that Joseph held Jesus's tiny body in his arms. Is he lacking

---

[282] Reference to Luke 2:46—it states that Joseph looked for Jesus for three days.

[283] Reference to Luke 2:46.

[284] Luke 2:48

[285] Luke 2:49

faith? All he feels right now is fear. The fear is taking all of his strength away; he knows he has to let Jesus go. His heart—it is thundering in his chest, and he cannot find any breath. Joseph's head is groggy, his body is going numb, his blood feels like ice, but his flesh feels on fire. Joseph begins collapsing to his knees, when Jesus grabs hold of his hands.

Joseph looks down one last time at his little boy and falls to his knees. He embraces his Son tightly with all the love of a grieving father. The Lord has asked Joseph to give Him back His Son. Joseph understands he will not see the end of this journey.[286] Joseph's tears are wet against Jesus's cheeks, and he whispers, "Father!"

All seems to stop around him, and there is stillness. He feels the Spirit come, like He did that first night.

"Son."

"Yahweh, please…"

"I know, you do not have to ask. I am here; I have always been here."

"I have not felt You."

"Because you are only choosing to feel your fear, and I do not dwell in fear. Finally, you broke away from it to call to Me."

"I cannot do this. Why did you choose me? I do not know how to do what You are asking of me."

"Be still; and know I am Lord. Just breathe."

"I do not know how to breathe right now. I cannot feel any breath in my lungs."

"Be still. My Spirit will be your breath."

"I need this to stop… I cannot let Him go yet… I have not had enough time with Him… I need Him still…"

"All you need is Me."

"I need to continue to protect Him. How can I let Him walk ahead of me alone?"

"I am here; He will never be alone."

---

[286] Joseph is not mentioned in the Bible again. Scholars believed he died before the crucifixion.

"But this place is not good enough for Him... this world will never love Him enough..."

"Son, stop arguing with me. My ways are perfect, this place is perfect, and My Son is perfect. Be still, and allow Me to enter into your heart so I can accomplish My plan."

Joseph becomes still and quiet, and the Holy Spirit comes upon him. Everything becomes holy. He pulls away from Jesus and sees Him for the first time. He looks around and sees the temple as Jesus's throne. He looks around and sees the land as Jesus's kingdom. He looks upon his little boy and sees God.

Joseph's journey is finished. He has questioned for so long "why him," and at this moment he finally learns why... because no one is capable of being His father, but him.

LOVE'S RECONCILIATION

Jesus entered Jericho and was passing through. A man was there by the name of Zacchaeus; he was a chief tax collector and was wealthy. He wanted to see who Jesus was, but because he was short, he could not see over the crowd. So he ran ahead and climbed a sycamore-fig tree to see him, since Jesus was coming that way. When Jesus reached the spot, he looked up and said to him, "Zacchaeus, come down immediately. I must stay at your house today." So he came down at once and welcomed him gladly. All the people saw this and began to mutter, "He has gone to be the guest of a sinner." But Zacchaeus stood up and said to the Lord, "Look, Lord! Here and now, I give half of my possessions to the poor, and if I have cheated anybody out of anything, I will pay back four times the amount." Jesus said to him, "Today salvation has come to this house, because this man, too, is a son of Abraham. For the Son of Man came to seek and to save the lost."

Luke 19:1-10

I revealed myself to those who did not ask for me; I was found by those who did not seek me.

Isaiah 65:1

Christ Jesus came into the world to save sinners—of whom I am the worst.
But for that very reason I was shown mercy so that in me, the worst of sin-
ners, Christ Jesus might display his immense patience as an example for those
who would believe in him and receive eternal life.

1 Timothy 1:15-16

But you are a chosen people, a royal priesthood, a holy nation, God's special
possession, that you may declare the praises of him who called you out of
darkness into his wonderful light. Once you were not a people, but now you
are the people of God; once you had not received mercy, but now you have
received mercy.

1 Peter 2:9-10

Every place he wanders he is hated. Every time he does his job people loathe and despise him. Every relationship is ruined; there is no
one left to love him. Instead of that annihilating him, Zacchaeus actually glories in it; he desires supremacy more than acceptance. His god is
power, and for years it fulfilled him. Until one day... this day... this day
it did not...

It is not a special day. Zacchaeus does not wake up with a new longing or a need for more. He wakes up the same as he always does: pomp-
ous and ready to walk over others. He takes the same route through
town that he always takes, but today it is filled with aggravation. Crowds
are everywhere. The people's presence turns his stomach. He has grown
to resent their existence. He has become their enemy and they are his,
and he is at peace with that. But today they block his path, he cannot
proceed, and the animosity boils within him.

He tries his best to move around them, to move through them, but
nothing is working. The resistance keeps coming and coming. A new
wave of people washes over him again and again, and he begins to feel
confused. Dizziness grows and he cannot make sense of his surroundings. He is lost, and he can no longer find his path.

Then in the distance he hears a voice. He tries to make out what the voice is saying, but he cannot hear. There is too much noise from the world surrounding him. He tries to look, but the crowds are too big and he cannot see over them. Zacchaeus hears the voice again. It is faint, but he thinks he hears his name being called. He suddenly wants to know, and see, who is in the center of the crowd. Zacchaeus suddenly wants it more than anything. He wants it so much that he looks for a way...

It was on the third day of creation that the Father created the trees. God walked to the spot where the sycamore needed to be placed.[287] He looked to the Son and said, "It needs to be right here. It needs to grow strong and reach high, so he can see Us. It needs to provide strength and protection and show our eternity and divinity."[288] The Son felt the excitement of creating the perfect surroundings for His meeting with Zacchaeus, and He took extra care creating this tree. Jesus took time crafting the bark. He created it to be resilient, with a hardened dark-gray layer, that will shed to reveal a beautiful soft layer, camouflaged with grays, greens, and browns. The personification of Zacchaeus. Each architectural detail of creation is formed for the child that will use it someday. The Son knew this tree would be everything to Zacchaeus. It would be the key to bring him to the Father. Zacchaeus will want to see the truth more than hold onto life's treasures. He will want it so much that he will climb for it...

Zacchaeus keeps hearing the voice, but cannot see who is speaking. He feels blind, and in his frustration, he rests against a tree. He looks around, searching for an answer, and then realizes the answer is right in front of him. There stands a large sycamore tree. The branches reach high, but begin low, and offer a staircase to climb. He walks

---

[287] The tree was actually a *Sycamore Fig: Ficus Sycomorus*. Archaeobotanists believe these trees can live from 2,000–9,000 years. It is hard to calculate their exact age because the trees lack growth rings.

[288] Sycamore trees in the Bible symbolize strength, protection, eternity, and divinity.

over to the tree and pauses. He is not a boy or a commoner; he is a man of great power and wealth. Climbing a tree is beneath him, he tells himself. He does not need to embarrass himself and climb to see where the voice is coming from, so he turns to walk away. But in that moment a conviction comes upon his heart like an attack. Zacchaeus grabs his chest and feels the air leaving his lungs. Suddenly, everything is crashing in on him. Not just the people, but his entire life is causing him to feel claustrophobic, questioning every decision he has ever made. He begins to shake and looks up at the tree again. He wants the climb; he needs it to breathe again. He wants to know who that voice belongs to more than anything else. Suddenly, power and riches are not enough. He knows they will not help him breathe again and escape this oppressive prison he calls his life. So he decides to climb the sycamore tree.

Zacchaeus climbs high; he does not want to risk not seeing the truth. When he reaches a spot high enough, he feels nervous to turn around to see beyond the crowds. It is an anticipation he has never felt before. Zacchaeus is nervous about what he will see. Will he still not be able to see who is speaking? Will he be disappointed? Or worse yet, will the One who is speaking see him? Shame begins to fill him, and he realizes he does not want to be seen the way he is. He is nothing but a little man, inside and out. He decides he will not turn around to look. He will climb back down and live the rest of his life wondering. That will be safer and better, and he can continue on with his life unchallenged. He will go back to his choices. After all, they brought him everything the world promised to give.

Zacchaeus starts to climb down with that lie in his head, when he feels the pain in his chest again. He realizes the pain is emptiness. He is empty. He is a small, empty shell of a man. He has tried his entire life to do things to get himself to grow bigger and be seen, but all of his choices have only made him smaller and smaller. For once he wants to be seen. For once he wants to feel love. He stops climbing down, turns around, and instantly he hears the voice call out...

"Zacchaeus! Quick, come down! For I must be a guest in your home today."[289]

The Spirit pushes air into Zacchaeus's lungs and he takes a breath; it is the sweetest air he has ever tasted. He looks, and the crowds part, as the Man walks toward the tree. Zacchaeus is confused. How does this Man know his name? Why is this Man calling out to him? What does the Man want with him? Zacchaeus is too small, he is too hated, and he is too despised to matter. Zacchaeus grips the tree tighter; he is too scared to let go. If he does, he may fall out of this dream he is in.

"Zacchaeus, I see you, please come down and be with Me. Let Me be a guest in your house."

"You want me? You must have me confused with someone else. You cannot want me."

"I am not mistaken; it is you I want."

"Do You know who I am? What I do?"

"Yes, I know you, Zacchaeus. I see you."

"If You see me, then You know I am small, and should be overlooked. You should move on to someone else."

"I do not want to move on; I have been waiting a long time for you. I want you, no one else."

"Why me?"

"Because you climbed a tree to see Me. Please come down, and let Me be a guest in your home."

Zacchaeus hangs onto the tree, frozen in place. What will having this Man as a guest at his home mean? If he invites the Man to his home, how will his life change? Should he risk that unknown? He thinks these things over as he examines the tree that is holding him. Zacchaeus feels the bark; it feels ancient to him, like the tree has always been here. Zacchaeus notices the nook he is sitting in fits his body perfectly, almost like it was created just for him. He does not understand

---

[289] Luke 19:5 NLT

why he needed to climb this tree, but off the ground, Zacchaeus can finally see the truth.

Zacchaeus knows the Man does not want to come into his home, but into his life. The Man has a plan and wants him to be part of it. Zacchaeus knows that for the first time he is seen and he is loved. Great joy and excitement fill his heart and mind, and Zacchaeus quickly climbs down.[290] He will take this Man into his home, and his home will know salvation, and Zacchaeus will never be lost again.[291]

---

[290] Reference to Luke 19:6.
[291] Reference to Luke 19:9-10.

LOVE'S SHEPHERDING

Then Jesus told them this parable: "Suppose one of you has a hundred sheep and loses one of them. Doesn't he leave the ninety-nine in the open country and go after the lost sheep until he finds it? And when he finds it, he joyfully puts it on his shoulders and goes home. Then he calls his friends and neighbors together and says, 'Rejoice with me; I have found my lost sheep.'
I tell you that in the same way there will be more rejoicing in heaven over one sinner who repents than over ninety-nine righteous persons who do not need to repent."

Luke 15:3-7

The sheep listen to his voice. He calls his own sheep by name and leads them out. When he has brought out all his own, he goes on ahead of them, and his sheep follow him because they know his voice. But they will never follow a stranger; in fact, they will run away from him because they do not recognize a stranger's voice... Therefore Jesus said again, "Very truly I tell you, I am the gate for the sheep. All who have come before me are thieves and robbers... I am the gate; whoever enters through me will be saved. They will come in and go out, and find pasture. The thief comes only to steal and kill and destroy; I have come that they may have life, and have it to the full... I am the good shepherd. The good shepherd lays down his life for the sheep...

*I am the good shepherd; I know my sheep and my sheep know
me—just as the Father knows me and I know the Father—and I lay down
my life for the sheep. I have other sheep that are not of this sheep pen.
I must bring them also. They too will listen to my voice, and there shall be
one flock and one shepherd. The reason my Father loves me is that I lay
down my life—only to take it up again. No one takes it from me,
but I lay it down of my own accord. I have authority to lay it down
and authority to take it up again.
This command I received from my Father."*

John 10:3-5, 7-11, 14-18

*He tends his flock like a shepherd: He gathers the lambs in his arms
and carries them close to his heart...*

Isaiah 40:11

Abel was the first. God ordained him to care for His sheep. A job as old as time. The Father knows no other job is more important. Moses... David... shepherding called so many. No lonelier or more despised job has ever been created.

There are no hours, no days, no weeks; there is just an eternal life of shepherding. It never begins and it never stops. The Shepherd creates a home for His sheep, surrounding their pasture with a protective wooden wall covered with thorns to keep the enemy away. Inside this haven, the sheep are safe. Inside, the sheep belong to the Shepherd. The Shepherd never uses dogs nipping at their bodies to herd His sheep, causing panic. The Shepherd never uses pain tactics to move His sheep on the right path. The Shepherd strives greatly to keep His sheep safe and without blemish. The Shepherd uses love and tenderness to teach His sheep His voice.[292] Day after day, night after night, the sheep hear

---

[292] Biblical shepherds did not use sticks, dogs, or any tools to manage their sheep. The sheep obeyed commands only from the shepherd's own voice.

the voice of their Shepherd leading them and guiding them on the right path. All other voices fall on deaf ears. In the midst of a sea of voices, the sheep only recognize their Shepherd's. When He calls, they will follow, never out of fear of dogs nipping at them, but trusting the nurturing love in the voice of their Shepherd.

Encased with their smell and grime on His body, the Shepherd repulses everyone who comes near. The stench of the sheep is too great for anyone but the Shepherd. He lovingly bathes each of them to make them clean. Then He lays His body down at the gate to protect them.[293] The entrance to the pasture is secure because His body will guard against the enemy. He will sleep stretched across the only gate in and out; His own life will be the only shield the sheep will ever need.

But sheep are prone to wander... and one little lamb goes astray. The little lamb begins eating grass. It tastes sweet and invites him to come back over and over again for more. The sweet grass satisfies his hunger. He has no intentions of going beyond the wall. He continues to eat aimlessly and without regard, and before he realizes it, he has eaten all that is within his pasture. It is not a choice, but a movement. The lamb does not even think about it, but he inches closer and closer toward the wall. He goes beyond the wall for only a moment. The lamb can still see the wall, so he thinks he is still safe. He will just stay close to the wall of the pasture; he will still be able to hear the Shepherd's voice, the lamb tells himself. He continues to eat. He moves slightly to the left, then to the right. There is more grass ahead of him; he will go just a little farther.

Finally, he is full and wants to sleep. He looks and sees no shelter. He looks to the left and he looks to the right. He looks ahead, he looks behind, and still sees nothing. No more grass, just nothing. There is nothing but mud and emptiness. The little lamb looks at himself and

---

[293] There was often no gate to keep or protect the sheep inside their pens; therefore, shepherds would sleep at the entrance to block any wild animals or thieves from coming in.

realizes he is now covered in mud. He feels so dirty and isolated. He stops and listens for the Shepherd's voice, but the nothingness drowns out all of the sound. How will he find his way home? How will he ever sleep again? He can only sleep with the security of knowing the Shepherd is at the gate. Now enemies of all kinds can reach the little lamb. Panic sets in. He has wandered off into the nothingness, and he is all alone without hope.

It is time to end the day, and put His sheep to bed. The Shepherd calls out for them to return to Him from their eating. He begins to count... 96... 97... 98... 99... He knows the little lamb that is gone. The Shepherd knows this little lamb is curious. He knows this little lamb is willful. He knows this little lamb is restless. But this little lamb has a yearning soul and has captured the Shepherd's heart. The Shepherd's love for the little lamb is all-consuming, and His only purpose. The Shepherd knows He has to make the journey to rescue the little lamb.

The Shepherd calls out for the little lamb, and realizes how far he has wandered. The Shepherd must go beyond the protective wall. The Shepherd must go through the thorns. The Shepherd climbs up the wood beams and reaches the thorns at the top. The Shepherd pushes through as the thorns pierce His skin and rip His flesh. Blood trickles down, but the Shepherd feels no pain, just determination. The Shepherd smells the sweet grass that tempted the little lamb, but as He walks on, He begins to smell the horrors of the nothingness. The farther the Shepherd walks on, the more His feet struggle to move through the thick and heavy mud. The Shepherd does not stop calling, constantly calling out for the little lamb to hear His voice as He walks.

The lambs hear the Shepherd's voice in the distance, and feels the salvation coming. He begins to run toward it, but quickly stops. The little lamb remembers that he is now so dirty. The Shepherd has always cared so tenderly for him, ensuring he is never blemished, and now he is covered with the residue of the place the Shepherd had always warned him about. The little lamb can never face the Shepherd this way, so he turns to walk away from the voice. The little lamb can never go back... he has wandered too far... those words are the song that echoes in his heart and mind. The little lamb decides to walk deeper into the nothingness.

The Shepherd sees the little lamb and begins to run toward him. The Shepherd's feet dig deep into the mud with devotion. The Shepherd ignores the breath that is not reaching His lungs, or the pain in His side, and He runs faster. The nothingness becomes darker, but He can still see His little lamb. The Shepherd thunders out a call one more time, filling the nothingness with His love. The little lamb stops.

The little lamb feels the nothingness shake underneath him, but he is too ashamed to turn around. The Shepherd approaches him with care. He reaches out and touches his dirty body. The little lamb recoils from His touch in embarrassment. The little lamb's once beautiful white coat is now dirty beyond cleansing; he does not want the Shepherd to see what he has done to his coat.

The Shepherd does not see the dirt that covers the lamb; He only sees the lamb He loves and misses so greatly. To the Shepherd, the little lamb is still perfect. The Shepherd bends down and embraces the little lamb in His arms. The Shepherd holds the lamb tight, crying tears of joy. The little lamb feels the love and acceptance in the Shepherd's arms and falls into His embrace. The little lamb does not understand how the Shepherd can be joyful about finding him after he disobeyed. But the Shepherd is crying because He has found him—*what kind of love is this*, the little lamb questions.

The Shepherd looks at the way the nothingness scarred His little lamb with mud and dirt. The Shepherd becomes angry at that mud and dirt—He resents the control it has over His little lamb's heart and mind. Never again will that happen. The Shepherd tells the little lamb to be still. He uses His hands to wipe the mud off, and the mud starts to leave the little lamb's body and fill the cracks and wrinkles of the Shepherd's hands again.[294] As the Shepherd continues to wipe, His blood from the thorns drips onto the little lamb's coat, staining it red. No words need to be spoken; the little lamb understands he can never wander so far away that the Shepherd cannot find him. The little lamb's coat now has the Shepherd's blood on it. It is the little lamb's mark; he is branded as the Shepherd's forever. The Shepherd lifts the little lamb to His shoulders and carries him back home.

---

[294] Reference to the story "Love at First Breath."

LOVE'S PEACE

That day when evening came, he said to his disciples, "Let us go over to the other side."
Leaving the crowd behind, they took him along, just as he was, in the boat. There were
also other boats with him. A furious squall came up, and the waves broke over the
boat, so that it was nearly swamped. Jesus was in the stern, sleeping on a cushion.
The disciples woke him and said to him, "Teacher, don't you care if we drown?" He got
up, rebuked the wind, and said to the waves, "Quiet! Be still!" Then the wind died down
and it was completely calm. He said to his disciples, "Why are you so afraid? Do
you still have no faith?"

Mark 4:35-41

I consider that our present sufferings are not worth comparing with the glory
that will be revealed in us.

Romans 8:18

There is no fear in love. But perfect love drives out fear, because fear has to do
with punishment. The one who fears is not made perfect in love.

1 John 4:18

Some went out on the sea in ships; they were merchants on the mighty waters.
They saw the works of the Lord, his wonderful deeds in the deep. For he spoke

and stirred up a tempest that lifted high the waves. They mounted up to the heavens and went down to the depths; in their peril their courage melted away. They reeled and staggered like drunkards; they were at their wits' end. Then they cried out to the Lord in their trouble, and he brought them out of their distress. He stilled the storm to a whisper; the waves of the sea were hushed.

Psalm 107:23-29

Though the mountains be shaken and the hills be removed, yet my unfailing love for you will not be shaken nor my covenant of peace be removed.

Isaiah 54:10

There is not an ache in His muscles, but a low throb. It started in His feet and ended between His eyes. A throb pulsating between His eyes that stretched out to His temples. Jesus's body is feeling the day wear on, and He needs rest. He looks out across the sea. He looks beyond the coming storm to see His glory. He knows the next path. He gathers His friends, and they set off on their journey in a boat that promises the rest He needs. The boat has seen many journeys before and has faced down many storms; it is a strong vessel. Jesus knows it is all they need.

Once on the boat, Jesus's human body is weak, and he seeks out a place below to sleep, for He is at peace. The others are not at peace. The others do not follow Jesus; they stay at the top to keep their eyes on the water. They see the gray skies coming and question how they could not see them before they left the shore. The storm is not predicted and is not prepared for. They have nothing on the boat to protect them. They begin to make their plans for survival. The disciples stay on the deck to fight the storm alone. Jesus goes below, and falls asleep alone in peace.

Before the disciples can take a breath, waves begin crashing into the boat, swallowing it like a little morsel, but not enough to satisfy its relentless hunger. The skies turn from gray to black, and the only light comes from the crashing lightning jabbing through the sky in rage. They cannot see or grab ahold of anything that may save their lives. In panic and fear, the disciples make plans with each other. Jesus sleeps.

Shouting through the echoes of the thunder, they try to navigate saving the vessel. Keep the bow into the sea at all costs. Keep a firm hand on the steerage; do not let the wheel get away. Drop the anchor; try to keep the waves from gaining control. Lower the sails; do not give the wind a chance to take the boat in another direction. Prepare for lightning strikes; avoid the fires. They are trying to do each step, but the storm is winning each battle. Jesus sleeps.

One of them realizes that Jesus is not with them, and his panic paralyzes him. Did Jesus fall overboard? Did Jesus get hurt? Did Jesus take His eyes off the horizon? Why was Jesus not there with them? The friends struggle against the waves, trying to look for Jesus. They cannot find Him anywhere. They are losing the war against the storm, and losing all of their energy to continue on with the fight. They decide to retreat down below in the belly of the boat. There they find Jesus asleep.

Anger grips the last bit of strength their bodies possess; how can Jesus sleep? He must not care. He must not love them. They try to yell over the storm.

"Teacher..."

Jesus still sleeps. Their anger fills them. They yell louder.

"Teacher..."

Jesus still sleeps. Their anger empties and fear fills their heart; they begin screaming.

"Teacher...Teacher do you not care that we are going to drown?"[295]

Jesus wakes.

Jesus is frustrated to be woken from His slumber. He looks at His friends wet and desperate in their fear. He moves beyond them

---

[295] Mark 4:38

without giving them a word. He moves with calm grace up to face the storm. Jesus goes to the top of the boat with His friends cautiously behind Him.

Jesus looks out at His creation and rebukes it, "Quiet! Be still!"[296]

The storm obeys, and it stops. The waves bow down in humble reverence, the thunder quiets, turning away like a scolded child. The lightning flickers out like a tiny candle, and with a wave of His hand, Jesus brushes away the black sky with the ease of brushing away a lock of hair. All on the boat look at Him in fearful awe. They do not know if His great power makes Him their savior or enemy. They whisper to each other.

"Who is this man, that even the wind and waves obey him?"[297]

Jesus knows they still do not understand, and He is frustrated.

"Why are you so afraid? Do you still not have faith in Me?"[298]

Jesus lifts His hand one more time without looking at the sky, and the sun begins to shine through the clouds. His friends can feel its warmth on their faces, but Jesus is still disheartened with their lack of trust.

"I did not want to go around that storm; I wanted to go through it."

The friends still do not understand.

"Go through it?" Their voices are weak, nervous to question Him. "Why would anyone want to go through a storm? Why invite that kind of danger? Why... why us... why are you putting us through the storm—we were dying. The storm was too great for us. Did You not understand that? Did You not understand how bad the waves were? They were pulling us deep down into the sea. Did You not understand how the thunder was pounding upon us? Did You not understand that the lightning was throwing daggers at us? Did You not understand that the wind stole our breath?"

---

[296] Mark 4:39
[297] Mark 4:41
[298] Mark 4:40

"Your breath? Who do you think is giving you breath right now?"

The disciples look confused, so Jesus continues on.

"It is my Father's Spirit that fills your lungs right now. Without the Spirit's breath you would not have the air in your lungs to call out to Me."

The disciples do not even take a moment to cherish that fact, but continue with their complaints.

"But You were going to let us drown..."

"Drown? What power can engulf Me?"

"But You were not with us; You left us alone."

"No. I never left; I have always been in this boat. You chose not to come with Me. You chose to keep your eyes focused on the storm instead of coming with Me to sleep."

"How could we sleep at a time like this? We were fighting for our lives!"

"Why?"

The friends are shocked at His innocent ignorance.

"Because we were battling a war, fighting the storm."

"It is not your storm to fight. It has always been My storm. This is My creation and you are My children. If you had allowed yourselves to go through it with Me instead of trying to control it, you would have seen My glory... you dropped your anchor, tried to steady your steering, you gathered your sails... everything, but come to Me. If you had followed Me and slept in faith, you would have seen My glory. You would have seen how My glory always rescues you. You would have understood My plan."

"But You were taking so long; the boat was sinking..."

"This boat is My Word; it will never sink. My Word will always guide and protect you in the storm. You should never fear the storm. Look at what it can bring."

His friends look out onto the sea and see the calmness. They look up to the sun and see the new life it is bringing with a new day. Jesus continues on.

"I wanted to go through the storm. The darkness of night always propels the day; you have to go through the storm to appreciate the peace afterward. You only see the storm's destruction. Like a barrier island taking a beating in a hurricane, you do not see anything good from it. But barrier islands need the hurricane to get replenished. Without the power of a hurricane, sand, nutrients, and sediment on the ocean's floor could never reach the barrier island. Without the storm's wind and waves, the island would get lost. It is the storm that moves it closer to the mainland. Without the storm, the barrier island would eventually shrink and sink into the ocean."

His friends are trying to let go of their fears to trust in what He is saying, but it is hard to be brave enough to face the storm. Jesus knows their doubts.

"When the waves pull you down, I will calm them and raise you up. When the thunder pounds down on you, I will hush the skies and bring the stars. When the lightning is throwing daggers, I will soothe your wounds and heal you. When the wind steals your breath, I will fill your lungs with My peaceful inspiration. Remember, when you feel like you will drown, I will silence the storm for you. I will always silence the storm if you come to Me. I never left the boat—stay with Me and take your eyes off the storm. I will never let the storm sink your barrier island if you come to Me. So again, I ask you, why were you so afraid?"

LOVE'S FORGIVENESS

When Jesus got out of the boat, a man with an impure spirit came from the tombs to meet him. This man lived in the tombs, and no one could bind him anymore, not even with a chain. For he had often been chained hand and foot, but he tore the chains apart and broke the irons on his feet. No one was strong enough to subdue him. Night and day among the tombs and in the hills, he would cry out and cut himself with stones. When he saw Jesus from a distance, he ran and fell on his knees in front of him. He shouted at the top of his voice, "What do you want with me, Jesus, Son of the Most High God? In God's name don't torture me!" For Jesus had said to him, "Come out of this man, you impure spirit!" Then Jesus asked him, "What is your name?" "My name is Legion," he replied, "for we are many... The demons begged Jesus, 'Send us among the pigs; allow us to go into them.' He gave them permission, and the impure spirits came out and went into the pigs. The herd, about two thousand in number, rushed down the steep bank into the lake and were drowned.... the people went out to see what had happened. When they came to Jesus, they saw the man who had been possessed by the legion of demons, sitting there, dressed and in his right mind...

Mark 5:2-9, 12-15

My dear children, I write this to you so that you will not sin. But if anybody does sin, we have an advocate with the Father—Jesus Christ, the Righteous One. He is the atoning sacrifice for our sins, and not only for ours, but also for the sins of the whole world.

1 John 2:1-2

He does not treat us as our sins deserve or repay us according to our iniquities. For as high as the heavens are above the earth, so great is his love for those who fear him; as far as the east is from the west, so far has he removed our transgressions from us. As a father has compassion on his children, so the LORD has compassion on those who fear him; for he knows how we are formed, he remembers that we are dust.

Psalm 103:10-14

The demons come in the form of a broken man. The demons come to meet Jesus with a challenge, not a plea. The others may have been confused about who Jesus is, but the demons know the Son of God by name. The demons have been battling Him since the beginning, and they understand their time is limited. They are not ready for Jesus to stop them right now, so the demons challenge Jesus by approaching Him. Jesus gives them permission to speak.[299]

"What do you want with me, Jesus..."[300]

Jesus looks through the man standing in front of Him. The demons shriek.

"Why are you bothering me, Jesus, Son of the Most High God?"[301]

Jesus remains silent. His presence is making the demons wince in pain.

"In God's name, do not torture me!"[302]

---

[299] In Job it is learned that Satan needs God's permission before he acts.

[300] Mark 5:6

[301] Mark 5:7

[302] Mark 5:7

Jesus can see there are many of them. Anger starts to grow within His Spirit. With firm eyes, Jesus commands His will.

"Come out of this man, you impure spirit!"[303]

The demons recoil and fall to their knees. They have no other choice; they are on the Creator's leash.

"What is your name?"[304]

"My name is Legion, for we are many."[305]

That is enough; Jesus's ears cannot bear to hear another word slither out of the demon's mouth. Jesus looks down at the earthly body of this man. The demons have abused it and used it as their playground for too long. Jesus looks through all of the demons to find the man at the bottom of his soul. He can see that long ago he felt alone, confused, and unloved. In that emptiness, the demons flirted and seduced him, promising lies. The man looked their direction for one moment, and that was all it took for the enemy to win his soul. It was such a small moment, a pause really, but for one moment, the man could not find his breath. Jesus sees the day it happened. It is a day the man has lived a hundred times over, but that day the man looked their way. There was no distraction that caused his eyes to wander, no noise that turned his head that direction—just one moment that he paused.

That day the demons circled him like vultures, but the man thought they were doves promising hope. Jesus sees the lies they fed him. They have been feeding him for years, keeping him in a prison inside his own body. A prison he has tried to escape, but the demons will not let him go. The demons rejoiced every time he cut himself to free himself of the chains, for it made the chains heavier. The demons rejoiced every time he cried out because it just made their worship louder. The demons rejoiced when he slept among the dead because it slowly killed him too. Now here is the corpse of a once-living man kneeling in front

---

[303] Mark 5:8
[304] Mark 5:9
[305] Mark 5:9

of Jesus, and His heart breaks. Jesus looks to the Father and knows He has to use these demons to defeat Satan.

Fear grips the demons—they know Jesus is going to send them back to hell. Either to the home of the Deceiver or to the hell of idleness... which hell is worse? They pray to Jesus to not condemn them.

"Son of God, do not send us to a distant place... we pray this of you."[306]

Jesus is silent.

They yell louder, "Son of God, do not send us away... it's not God's appointed time yet."[307]

Jesus is silent.

"If you cast us out, send us into that herd of pigs," they beg. Tormenting swine is better than the abyss.[308]

With a wave of His hand, Jesus casts all the demons out of the man. He sends them into the herd of swine, and then to their watery death. He sends the pigs into the sea He just tamed.[309] The waters that choked the boat are now choking the life out of the pigs. The agonized cries of the demons fill the sky; the agony from God meeting evil with love.

When the demons leave, only a shell of the man is left. The shell collapses onto the ground. The man's naked, broken body has nothing left to hide. All of his scars, cuts, and blood are there for Jesus to see. He tries to cover himself, but his shame is too exposed.

"Why? Why did You do that for me?"

"Because you are worthy of it."

"I am not worthy of anything."

"You do not understand My judgment of worth. Would you like to leave this place?"

---

[306] Mark 5:10

[307] Matthew 8:29

[308] Mark 5:12

[309] Reference to Mark 5:13. This event happened just after Jesus calmed the storm with the disciples.

"I cannot leave. I have tried to break free from their prison, but even when I broke the chains I could never escape. Nothing will release me. I live among the decaying dead because I am decaying and dead too. I cut myself to give evidence that I still exist, but even then it is not enough for them. My body is graffiti with the Deceiver's mark. These cuts are his signature on my soul. Many would try to restrain me to lead me away... they would put me into shackles, but no one was ever strong enough to hold me."

"I can hold you."

"No, nothing can touch me; I am too spoiled. My body is a putrid shell, my lungs have atrophied, and I can no longer breathe."

"Allow Me to breathe for you."

"It is too late."

"What is your name?"

"I no longer know. I do not remember a time when I was not Legion. That is who I am."

"No."

"How can I have a name? Those demons did more than fill me, they became me and I them. I accepted those demons into my heart. No one has ever been able to overcome the Deceiver's power. He told me I do not have a name, so I no longer have a name."

Jesus comes closer to the man. Jesus takes His cloak off His shoulders and wraps it around him. The man looks up with tears in his eyes. He has not felt the warmth of clothing in so long.

"I created you with a name."

The man turns away. Jesus sits next to him and continues.

"You are not alone. All my children have demons in them. All have the scars that the Deceiver has branded on their bodies. Some can be covered and some cannot, but they are there... I see them all. My Father sent me so I can approach the demons for Him. I will turn the demons' evil into God's glory."

The man listens to this quietly. He almost believes; he wants to believe and hope for more, but then he looks at his scars again.

"I cannot be used for glory."

"You can be used for My glorious plan. Your worth is in your name, please let Me give it to you."

"There is nothing left of me for You to give anything."

"There is nothing left of you, but I want to recreate you. I want to give you your name. You were never strong enough to break the chains and walk away. The Deceiver was giving you strength, and he was not created to have the power to release the demons and redeem you. The Deceiver only has weakness that he uses to control, and I offer strength to give life and freedom. I will be your strength."

"How can you give me a name?"

"The scars of the demons you carry inside can only be healed, and you transformed, by recognizing that you are loved."

The man does not understand. No one has ever loved him before. He laughs at the absurdity of it all.

"Who will love me? Look at me! Look at what I have created! I am evil."

"I am offering you My love. I offer the evil in you My forgiveness as a gesture of My love. If you will accept it, then the demons and scars will go away and never come back. Then I will give you your name."

The man does not know what to say. He has lived with his demons for so long; they have become the only comfort he has. Now this Man is asking him to change, to let it all go. If he lets go of the demons, what will he be? Is there anything left of him to be anything else, he questions? Why does this Man want to love him? Why does He come to him? What if he lets go and allows this Man to love him, and then he fails? What if he cannot be the person this Man's love deserves? Would the Man leave him? No, it is too much to risk; it is safer for the man to stay and just die. Jesus hears the man's troubled heart.

"I will never leave you. My hope is forever. My love is forever. My plan is forever, and if you accept me right now, you will be a part of My plan."

"I have nothing to give You."

"You do not see... I have not come for anything you can give, but only to give you Me."

The man feels the warm cloak around his body. The cloth of it does not scratch or rub his scars, but feels like a healing bandage. He takes in the smell of it, breathing it in. It feels like the first breath of fresh air he has ever had; it is the breath of the Spirit. The Spirit enters him, and for the first time he sees a glimmer of hope for a different life. Just a glimmer is enough to give him the strength to look up. He looks to Jesus, and knows it is time to get dressed and leave this place behind.

"I want to know my name."

LOVE'S TEARS

On his arrival, Jesus found that Lazarus had already been in the tomb
for four days... "Lord," Martha said to Jesus, "if you had been here, my
brother would not have died. But I know that even now God will give you
whatever you ask" ... Jesus said to her, "Your brother will rise again." ...
Jesus said to her, "I am the resurrection and the life. The one who believes
in me will live, even though they die; and whoever lives by believing in me
will never die. Do you believe this?" ...When Mary reached the place
where Jesus was and saw him, she fell at his feet and said, "Lord, if you
had been here, my brother would not have died." ...When Jesus saw her
weeping, and the Jews who had come along with her also weeping, he was
deeply moved in spirit and troubled. "Where have you laid him?" he asked.
"Come and see, Lord," they replied. Jesus wept.

John 11:17, 21-23, 25-26, 32-35

Come to me, all who labor and are heavy laden, and I will give you rest. Take
my yoke upon you, and learn from me, for I am gentle and lowly in heart, and
you will find rest for your souls. For my yoke is easy, and my burden is light.

Matthew 11:28-30

The Lord your God in your midst, The Mighty One, will save; He will rejoice over you with gladness, He will quiet you with His love, He will rejoice over you with singing.

Zephaniah 3:17 KJV

Empathy. Empathy and love are the only things behind His tears. Jesus weeps with His friends. Jesus cries with them because He carries their pain and feels their sorrow. Jesus is not grieving death with them. He knows death does not really exist. But for them it does, and He honors that with His tears now. Jesus is grieving the heartache His friends feel right now in this moment. Jesus wants to bear their pain because they are His children who He loves. Jesus wants to carry their torment, because that is His only purpose. Jesus weeps.

Empathy. Empathy for the shock that has taken hold of their bodies right now. Jesus sees the shock is taking away their breath. They are trying to breath, but they cannot find the air. He grabs hold of their hands and feels the coldness left from the fragmented remnants that were once their souls. Jesus weeps.

Empathy. Empathy for the pain. Jesus knows they cannot see beyond their anguish right now. They cannot see the miracle that is about to happen. They cannot see tomorrow. Jesus knows they do not understand this pain will be so short in their lives. He knows they will measure time by this pain. They will sit in it and let it absorb each minute of their lives. Jesus knows they do not understand He is about to take all the pain away. They only know of this moment, and in this moment, they feel agony down to their bones. Jesus weeps.

Empathy. Empathy to answer their screams of "why." The anger demands that answer now. They are clinging to Him—pounding and begging for Him to explain this grief. They want to fight everything, to make the whole world feel the pain they are feeling right now. Through their tears, they look to Jesus and want to fight Him. He came too late.

He could have stopped this, but He did not. He allowed it. But the anger is not bigger than the pain, and they do not have enough fight. All they have are the tears. Jesus weeps.

Empathy. Empathy for the sadness. Jesus knows that in this moment all His friends can do is cry. There is no room for faith. There is no room for praises. The pain is filling up every corner of their hearts, and there is no more room for anything else. Jesus weeps.

Jesus does not need to weep; He is in control, but still He weeps. The Three have been planning for this moment for a long time, and have prepared a plan to comfort them. Jesus feels the pain Mary and Martha are feeling. Jesus knows in a matter of minutes a miracle will happen, but minutes feel like a lifetime to them. Jesus weeps. This moment is all Mary and Martha know; time has stopped for them. So Jesus stops with them and weeps. Jesus weeps with them now because He loves His children. Jesus weeps with them now because it is only through tears that eyes can focus on salvation. This human death is not beyond the Father's plan. This human death is not beyond the Father's love. And these tears are not beyond the Father's glory.

Jesus commands, "Take the stone away."[310]

---

[310] John 11:39

LOVE'S RANSOM

*Jesus knew that his hour had come to leave this world and return to his
Father. He had loved his disciples during his ministry on earth, and now he
loved them to the very end. It was time for supper, and the devil had already
prompted Judas, son of Simon Iscariot, to betray Jesus. Jesus knew that the
Father had given him authority over everything and that he had come from
God and would return to God. So he got up from the table, took off his robe,
wrapped a towel around his waist, and poured water into a basin. Then he
began to wash the disciples' feet, drying them with the towel he had around
him... "I am not saying these things to all of you; I know the ones
I have chosen. But this fulfills the Scripture that says, 'The one who eats
my food has turned against me.' I tell you this beforehand, so that when it
happens you will believe that I am the Messiah"... Now Jesus was deeply
troubled, and he exclaimed, "I tell you the truth, one of you will betray me!...
It is the one to whom I give the bread I dip in the bowl."
And when he had dipped it, he gave it to Judas, son of Simon Iscariot.
When Judas had eaten the bread, Satan entered into him. Then Jesus told
him, "Hurry and do what you're going to do."*

John 13:1-5, 18-19, 21, 26-27 NLT

But I am afraid that just as Eve was deceived by the serpent's cunning, your minds may somehow be led astray from your sincere and pure devotion to Christ.

2 Corinthians 11:3

For in him all things were created: things in heaven and on earth, visible and invisible, whether thrones or powers or rulers or authorities; all things have been created through him and for him. He is before all things, and in him all things hold together.

Colossians 1:16-17

But as for you, you meant evil against me; but God meant it for good, in order to bring it about as it is this day, to save many people alive.

Genesis 50:20 NKJV

Even my own familiar friend in whom I trusted, Who ate my bread, Has lifted up his heel against me.

Psalm 41:9 NKJV

Jesus knows this is the moment to show them the full extent of His love. To the twelve this is just another celebration, but to Jesus this is a ceremony of devotion.[311] Another long day of feasting, remembering the past, and walking far, covering their feet with earth. Twelve pairs of feet covered in the ancient dirt, filthy with the mud of what is to come. Jesus looks at their surprised faces as He bends down with the bowl to clean those feet. The disciples are not sure what is happening; surely, He does not mean to wash their feet? A service for the lowliest of servants. Some disciples feel regret in their hearts for not thinking first to wash His feet. Jesus sees the confusion in their hearts. He tries to explain that the answers will come soon.

---

[311] The Last Supper happened during the Jewish celebration of Passover.

"You do not understand now why I am doing it; someday you will."[312]

Many of them protest and insist that He should never serve them, but Jesus lovingly explains... [313]

"If I do not wash you, then you will not belong to Me."[314]

Even though the twelve do not understand, they concede and allow Jesus to serve them. As He looks at the mud that has hardened on their feet, He remembers the mud that hardened on His hands during creation. Sacrifice and love have been Jesus's only mission since the beginning.

Jesus uses care with each of them. He wants to make sure their feet are completely clean. The disciples do not understand why He wants to make them clean. All of it... all of the miracles, prayers, sermons... they are all with the intention of making them clean. The plan is so simple—to make God's children clean so they can live with Him again.

Jesus spends time with each of them, ordaining and commissioning them to carry on without Him. He saves Judas for last. As He approaches Judas, His heart becomes heavy. For three years, He has loved Judas. Jesus has given Judas opportunity after opportunity to choose another path...

The plan has been written since the beginning; the Father has ordained it. Jesus only came down from His Father's side to die. It will happen no matter what path or the person appointing it—the plan is commissioned by the Father. Jesus chose Judas to be one of His own because of love. Jesus knew of the prophecy, but wanted to give Judas another way.[315] He persistently endeavored over the past three years to give Judas another choice. Time and time again, Jesus encouraged

---

[312] John 13:7

[313] Reference to John 13:8.

[314] John 13:8

[315] Reference to Genesis 3:15.

Judas to reproach himself. Time and time again He loved Judas. But every time Jesus called Judas to come, another was calling him too. Judas was not created to be a man of evil, but to be a child of God. Jesus called Judas to be a part of His twelve to show him this gospel. But the Deceiver was always there whispering into Judas's soul. Like a termite eating its way into his mind, the Deceiver corrupted Judas with just suggestions. Suggestions of ego and pride turned into hatred and darkness...

Now Judas is sitting before Jesus, and His heart is troubled. Jesus's heart is heavy with the unrequited love Judas never showed Him. Jesus's heart is heavy over the sin and darkness that sits before Him. Sin embodies Judas; Jesus can see Satan sitting next to him as the puppet master. He looks to Judas, knowing that in his naivety of sin, he does not realize he has written his own death. Judas has become the infinite paradigm of the casualties of sin. But mostly Jesus's heart is heavy because He knows Judas is about to face eternity without the Father. Because of that, Jesus washes Judas's feet. It is the last moment He can show Judas love.

Judas's feet are especially dirty. It takes Jesus longer than with the rest to wash him. Mud reaches up his legs. It is dark and thick. Jesus's cloth quickly becomes black with the muck, and His basin of water congeals with the mire. Satan's face is filled with glee; excited anticipation fills him. Jesus does not take His eyes off of Satan while He washes Judas. Jesus does not allow Satan to speak; His stare says all that is needed. Now is the time for washing. When Jesus finishes, He knows it is time to begin the plan. Jesus looks directly to Satan and speaks.

"He who eats My bread has lifted up his heel against Me. From now on I am telling you before it comes to pass, so that when it does occur, you may believe that I am the Messiah."[316]

---

[316] John 13:18-20 NKJV

The Deceiver coils down in fear. Then with a broken heart, Jesus looks back to Judas and utters, "One of you will betray me."[317]

Jesus does not look to see the shocked unbelief on the disciples' faces. He knows they are feeling violated and questioning each other. Their friendships have been so close and trusting; who would dare plot against their Christ now? Who would become their enemy? As they interrogate each other, Jesus is lost in His thoughts. Jesus looks to Judas, and then He sees the smile on Satan's face. Jesus knows the Devil will not leave Him tonight. Satan wants to scream out his empty temptations, but Jesus already knows the answers. The Devil is trying to tempt Jesus with the haunting question that torments the heart. Why Judas? Why one of His beloved disciples? Why not one of His many enemies? Why one that has walked with Him?

The Devil believes he has challenged Jesus, and his smirk becomes bigger. But Jesus' stare quickly removes the smirk. The disciples look to Jesus in wonder; they have never seen this enmity before in His eyes. They look around the room, but cannot find the source of His intention. They are seeing Jesus differently; His presence seems to be filling the entire room. Jesus' Spirit seems to be growing larger and larger, towering over all of them. The disciples have seen many miracles, but none of them compared to the supernatural giant they are seeing in Him tonight.

In awe, the disciples plead with Him, and assure Jesus of the confidence of their love and honor for Him, but Judas stands there cold. Judas is no longer his own man, and he simply returns Jesus' stare. Judas's heart has changed, and the Man he once followed is now his nemesis. As Jesus looks at him, He can hear Judas's thoughts and knows any light that was once in him is now gone. Judas was not born for this, but chooses it freely. The Father did not will this for Judas, but He is allowing him to choose it. Judas Iscariot chooses to be Satan's instrument.

---

[317] John 13:21 NKJV

Judas was not designed to be evil and betray, but he chose darkness over light. Therefore, God takes Judas's betrayal and fits it into His plan to bring light to all of the world.

Jesus calms the disciples' distress and says, "It is the one to whom I give the bread dipped in the wine."[318]

Jesus dips the bread into the bowl and holds it out to Judas. In that moment, the Holy Spirit comes to give Judas one last chance. The Holy Spirit stands before Judas and breathes out. The Devil moves between the Holy Spirit and Judas, he crucifies the breath… the Devil smiles at Jesus… Judas takes the bread and eats, and the Devil enters him. All of the demons rejoice. It is finished; Judas is lost. Judas becomes a part of Satan. Jesus can no longer see his disciple Judas before him, but only the Devil.

Jesus looks away, and tears fill His eyes.

Judas never had Jesus fooled; He always knew the capability of Judas's impostor's heart. Jesus is not the victim to any man or to the Deceiver. This is the plan. The Devil does not understand that now, and poor Judas will never know what the plan really was. Thirty pieces of silver was not the betrayal of Jesus's life, but of Judas's.[319] For only thirty pieces of silver, Judas sold his own soul.

For all of Judas's treachery and hypocrisy, Jesus is not finished serving him. He sends Judas away to fulfill his job, and Jesus will walk willingly to the cross for Judas's sins… because that is love.

---

[318] John 13:26 NKJV

[319] Judas was paid thirty pieces of silver to betray Jesus.

LOVE'S PLAN

While he was still speaking a crowd came up, and the man who was
called Judas, one of the Twelve, was leading them. He approached Jesus
to kiss him, but Jesus asked him, "Judas, are you betraying the Son of
Man with a kiss?" When Jesus's followers saw what was
going to happen, they said, "Lord, should we strike with our swords?"
And one of them struck the servant of the high priest,
cutting off his right ear. But Jesus answered, "No more of this!"
And he touched the man's ear and healed him.

Luke 22:47-51

Surely, he took up our pain and bore our suffering, yet we considered him
punished by God, stricken by him, and afflicted. But he was pierced for our
transgressions; he was crushed for our iniquities; the punishment that brought
us peace was on him, and by his wounds we are healed. We all, like sheep,
have gone astray, and each of us has turned to our own way; and the Lord
has laid on him the iniquity of us all. He was oppressed and afflicted; yet
he did not open his mouth; he was led like a lamb to the slaughter; and as a
sheep before its shearers is silent, so he did not open his mouth.

Isaiah 53:4-7

The Servant immediately loses his balance and falls to the ground. Everything begins to spin around him, and he is instantly confused. He sees the sword come down upon his head, but he cannot feel pain, just numbness. He can feel warm, thick blood stream down his cheek and neck, so he knows the sword made contact. He looks to his side and sees his ear on the ground. He looks up to see the men fighting and screaming at each other, but all sound seems so far away. Everything seems to stop, and he looks around to his fellow servants and the guards, but no one seems to care about him. The Servant has served faithfully next to them for years, but now they seem like strangers. They are continuing on with their jobs, they are wrestling the others to the ground, and using rage as their weapons. Only One is looking at him—the One they came to arrest.

The Man is staring down at him. He is looking at no one else, just him broken on the ground. The Servant quickly becomes aware of his shame. He realizes he does not even know the crime the Man has committed that caused him to be sent here. The Servant was blindly following orders from the powers to whom he has pledged his allegiance. Now this Man is the only one who is concerned, and the rest would gladly let his body lie there in decay without any conviction. Then, against all the soldiers holding the Man back, He bends down to the Servant. The scene stops in awe, and for the first time all eyes are on the injured Servant on the ground.

Jesus feels compassion and pity for the Servant. He bends down, and with gentle eyes, assures him all will be corrected. In the brief moment Jesus looks into the Servant's eyes, He sees everything that is to come.

Jesus sees the farce of a trial, full of ignorance and pride. A trial that will turn followers into enemies. The cries of "Hosanna" will turn into cries of "Crucify Him," and they will ring in Jesus's ears. A trial that will never prove guilt, but will not reveal the truth to the blind either.

Jesus sees the beatings upon beatings to His body. Lashes across His back: thirty-nine—just one less from death. Flagrums, whips, and chains will condemn His body for the world's sin.[320] Shards of metal licking His back; ripping His flesh open. The whips will ravage His body, devouring the tissue over and...

over,

over,

over,

over,

over,

over,

over,

over,

over,

over,

over,

over,

over,

over,

over,

over,

over,

over,

over,

over,

over,

over,

over,

over,

over,

---

[320] Flagrums are scourging whips used by Roman soldiers. They were lead-tipped whips.

over,

over,

over,

over,

over,

over,

over,

over,

over,

over,

and over again.

Jesus can feel the crown of thorns that will be crushed upon His head. Long and piercing, the thorns will puncture His head all around. Each thorn will hit a fragile nerve, causing intense, maddening pain to overcome His face. Blood will flow down into His eyes creating stinging blindness. A crown from a sinful world rejecting the only King that can ever save them. A crown representing the extent of love they have for Him.

Jesus sees the heaviness of the cross. It will rub His broken body for miles, causing His wounds to fill with agony at every movement. Shards of wood will penetrate into each lesion, creating a new assault on His body. The blood loss will cause every muscle to become weak and pathetic. He sees that He will struggle to carry the sins of the world on His back. It will be a long walk, and His human body will barely endure it. Jesus will repeat to Himself, "Just carry the wood" for miles and miles.

Jesus can hear the echoing bang of the hammer coming down upon the nails that will pierce His hands and feet. The nails will penetrate through His skin, splintering veins and muscles into shreds. He will scream out in human agony, while His feet crush under the force of the rusty nails. Nails that have been used to crucify so many before Him; He will feel the blood of those previously convicted mix with His. Their transgressions will flow into His system.

Jesus feels His lungs gasping for air as He hangs there. For hours He will cry out for the Spirit to fill His lungs with breath, but breath will never come. To take a breath He will have to push up on His feet to just get a wisp of air into His lungs. With every push, His hands and feet will rip more. They will physically fall apart, and His lungs will become hard and dry, unable to expand. The blood will begin to fill His lungs, and put pressure around His broken heart. But He will push up seven times, risking His heart bursting to pieces to speak words of love and forgiveness.[321]

Jesus sees and feels all of this as He looks into the Servant's eyes and in this moment, He only feels love for the Servant. He smiles. Jesus picks up the Servant's ear, touches it to his head, and declares, "No more of this!"[322]

Jesus's touch is gentle and assuring, and the Servant leans into it as Jesus whispers. The Servant understands that this is not a healing; this is just a repair, and his soul longs for the true healing. The Servant wants to ask all of the questions his soul is screaming out at this moment, but Jesus quiets him.

"Shh... do not ask why; My Father's plan is perfect." Jesus smiles again. "Death is swallowed up in victory."[323]

The Servant wants to say something, but does not know what to express. Then the moment is over; Jesus stands and goes with the guards without arguing or fighting, just in peace. As the Servant watches Jesus walk away into the night, he knows he has just witnessed the beginning, not the end of Him. Then the Servant begins to hear for the first time. It starts softly, but gains grandeur. It is beautiful, and brings tears to his eyes. He hears singing, as if a chorus of rejoicing... as if all of heaven and creation are rejoicing as the Man walks away to His destiny.

---

[321] Jesus speaks seven times while on the cross.

[322] Luke 22:51

[323] 1 Corinthians 15:54

LOVE'S CHOSEN

Now in the sixth month the angel Gabriel was sent by God to a city of Galilee named Nazareth, to a virgin betrothed to a man whose name was Joseph, of the house of David. The virgin's name was Mary. And having come in, the angel said to her, "Rejoice, highly favored one, the Lord is with you; blessed are you among women!" But when she saw him, she was troubled at his saying, and considered what manner of greeting this was. Then the angel said to her, "Do not be afraid, Mary, for you have found favor with God. And behold, you will conceive in your womb and bring forth a Son, and shall call His name Jesus. He will be great, and will be called the Son of the Highest; and the Lord God will give Him the throne of His father David. And He will reign over the house of Jacob forever, and of His kingdom there will be no end." Then Mary said to the angel, "How can this be, since I do not know a man?" And the angel answered and said to her, "The Holy Spirit will come upon you, and the power of the Highest will overshadow you; therefore, also, that Holy One who is to be born will be called the Son of God. Now indeed, Elizabeth your relative has also conceived a son in her old age; and this is now the sixth month for her who was called barren. For with God nothing will be impossible." Then Mary said, "Behold the maidservant of the Lord! Let it be to me according to your word." And the angel departed from her.

Luke 1:26-38 NKJV

Joseph also went up from Galilee, out of the city of Nazareth, into Judea, to the city of David, which is called Bethlehem, because he was of the house and lineage of David, to be registered with Mary, his betrothed wife, who was with child. So it was, that while they were there, the days were completed for her to be delivered. And she brought forth her firstborn Son, and wrapped Him in swaddling cloths, and laid Him in a manger, because there was no room for them in the inn.

Luke 2:4-7 NKJV

Near the cross of Jesus stood his mother... When Jesus saw his mother there, and the disciple whom he loved standing nearby, he said to her, "Woman, here is your son," and to the disciple, "Here is your mother." From that time on, this disciple took her into his home.

John 19:25-27

So do not fear, for I am with you; do not be dismayed, for I am your God. I will strengthen you and help you; I will uphold you with my righteous right hand.

Isaiah 41:10

Now is your time of grief, but I will see you again and you will rejoice, and no one will take away your joy.

John 16:22

Mary looks down at her swollen belly. She wonders if He questions His choice in her. Mary does not fully understand what the future holds, but she understands that she is not able to do what Yahweh is asking of her. She is just a girl; she does not know how to be a mother. She has been praying silently in her heart for months that He would take this all away, but instead the baby grows larger and larger. Now there is no more room for Him to kick. She knows the baby is coming soon, and she is full of fear.

Mary is cold and weary. Does the Father look down upon her now and feel disappointment? Does He wish He had chosen someone wiser? *Why did not He choose someone wiser*, she questions? The night is getting darker, and the stars are peeping out of the black blanket of sky.

She looks to Joseph and feels guilt. How is he ever supposed to love a child that is not his? Does he love her or is he only here out of duty? Does she love him? She has never asked herself that before. He was chosen for her, and she just trusted that without question. Now she is questioning everything. She feels so alone at this moment. Joseph feels like a stranger, and she has been looking for her Father for days and has not found Him. Her back begins to ache.

They have been traveling for days. Long days. Her body wants a bed. For every new pain, her fears grow larger like her belly. Mary fears everything... the physical pain... will there be dangers with the labor? If He is God, then how does she hold Him? Will she hurt Him if she does not do it right? Will she be capable of loving Him like a true mother? Is she worthy to love Him? Can she teach Him anything? Will she ever be able to pass on motherly wisdom? What is her role in His life? Is she just a vessel and no more? There are too many questions; her head hurts. Mary's back tightens.

Mary offered all she is to the Lord, and now He leaves her in silence. She feels so weak, and she is begging the Lord for strength. Why did the Father choose her? The Lord must have made a mistake, Mary tells herself. Mary's thoughts are interrupted when she feels pressure in her lower back and around her stomach. She loses her breath. But they must go on. They have been going on for miles, and she knows she has to go on for as long as the Lord commands. This journey is just beginning for her.

Hours pass, and the pressure is getting greater; she can barely breathe. He is coming tonight, she feels it. She looks up, desperate. The night is so quiet and still, she cannot imagine it being broken by the cries of a baby. Suddenly, Mary feels cold and wet; she looks down and sees water and blood. Before she can find a breath in her lungs, she feels Joseph cradle her in his arms. She hears panic in his voice, but his arms feel strong. She cannot see anything; she can only look up. Her pain is very intense now; she needs a bed. Mary does not have the breath to ask for His help; she just trusts that the Father knows.

Mary cannot focus her eyes to see where she is being placed, but she feels Joseph lay her down on damp, moldy, and scratchy hay. As she takes a breath, foul odors of animals fill her nose. The smells make her feel sick. She cannot hold it back, and she throws up all over herself. She is embarrassed, but the pain is too great for her to worry about it. Mary feels the need to fight the pain—she thinks if she can only breathe through it, it will end. She tries, but it is exhausting her. She looks down and sees blood. The spasms are hitting her relentlessly like a hammer coming down. Mary looks up. Why did He choose her? She is not capable of this; she knows it, why does He not seem to realize it? Tears begin to roll down her cheeks. None of this feels right. How can this be a part of His plan? It is just a stable, barely fit for animals— how can this be the Father's plan for His Son? She feels so confused and abandoned.

She looks to Joseph; he is doing everything so calmly. He cleans her mouth and pulls her hair back away from her sweaty brow. Does the smell not bother him? Does he not doubt God's plan? Does he not feel like a stable is no place for the King to enter this world? Did God tell Joseph something different? Does he have more faith? Is she lacking faith? All she feels right now is fear sapping her strength. She knows she has to let fear go. She has to use her faith to survive this. Finally, she screams out, "Father."

All seems to stop around her, and there is stillness. She feels the Spirit come, like He did that first night.[324]

"Daughter."

---

[324] Reference to Luke 1:26–28.

"Yahweh, please..."

"I know, you do not have to ask. I am here; I have always been here."

"I have not felt You."

"Because you are only choosing to feel your fear, and I do not dwell in fear. Finally, you broke away from it to call to Me."

"I cannot do this. Why did You choose me? I do not know how to do what You are asking of me."

"Be still, and know I am Lord. Just breathe."

"I do not know how to breathe right now. I cannot feel any breath in my lungs."

"Be still; My Spirit will be your breath."

"I need a clean place... a bed... someone to help me to do this..."

"All you need is Me."

"This is not a righteous place for His birth... He needs a holy place..."

"I am here; this is a holy place. No other place will do."

"But..."

"Daughter, stop arguing with Me. My ways are perfect, this place is perfect, and My Son is perfect. Be still, and allow Me to enter into your heart so I can accomplish My plan."

She becomes still and quiet, and the Holy Spirit comes upon her. The Spirit fills her lungs, and Mary breathes Him in. Everything becomes holy. She looks around and sees the stable differently—it is sacred ground now. Mary looks to Joseph and sees him working so tenderly to be gentle with her, and she feels love. He was chosen for her because only he can be the man who can provide what she will need to walk on this path. Only Joseph is strong enough, and she is falling in genuine love with him tonight. Mary looks down upon her bare stomach and legs and feels power. The pain is still there, but she is no longer in fear of it. Joseph braces himself behind her body for support, and wraps his arms around her. Mary takes a deep breath and pushes...

...The pushing... the pushing of the crowds is overwhelming her. Mary pushes through the crowds of people. The streets of Jerusalem are overflowing with people coming for Passover.[325] She has not been this scared of the crowds in twenty-one years. Mary can still remember frantically searching for Jesus back then through these streets. Joseph was so strong, but she could not even breathe that day. Now she will lose Jesus again in Jerusalem, and again, she cannot breathe. How could so many people be here for this spectacle? It is like a sea of snakes covering the streets. Serpents have been following Jesus from the beginning, trying to kill the plan.[326] They should all be ashamed of themselves. How can the Father allow this? How is this part of His plan? Why did the Father choose her? She still is not capable of this. How is she supposed to watch her Son die? She has been praying silently in her heart that the Lord will take this all away, but instead the crowds grow larger and larger. She does not understand what is coming in the future, but she understands she is not able to do what He is asking of her now. The Father is asking her to be Jesus's mother and stand with Him. She is Jesus's mother; how can she stand there and not protect Him? Long ago, she questioned if she could be His mother and protect Him, but everything she ever needed to do came to her. It came every day for thirty-three years. She held Him at every fall and comforted His heart, and now she cannot hold Him for this fall. Mary is full of fear. She begins to sweat.

Mary is cold and weary. Does the Father look down upon her now and feel disappointment? Does He wish He had chosen someone wiser? Why did He not choose someone wiser, she questions.

Mary fears everything. The physical pain... will Jesus's human body feel this pain? He is God, but her little boy too. Will she be wrong if she fights for Him? Her servant's heart is calling her to worship Him, but her mother's love is saying that she has to fight. Mary has spent years teaching Him the ways of the world, but is He teaching her the ways of God now? Can Mary listen? She once questioned what her role should

---

[325] Jesus was crucified over Passover weekend.
[326] Reference to the serpent in the garden of Eden.

be in His life, but now she knows she was created to be His mother fully and completely. Mary's chest tightens.

She offered all she was to the Lord, and now He leaves her in silence. She feels so weak and is begging the Lord for strength. Why did He choose her? Mary feels pressure around her heart. She loses her breath. But they must go on. They have been going on for miles, and she knows she has to go on for as long as the Lord commands. This journey is just beginning for her. Hours pass and the pressure is getting greater. It will happen tonight; she feels it. Mary looks up, desperate. The night is so quiet and still, she cannot imagine it being broken by the cries of her baby. Suddenly they take Jesus away again. Before she can find a breath in her lungs, she feels John's hands grabbing her. He guides her through the crowds again. She hears panic in John's voice, but his arms feel strong. She cannot see anything; she can only look up. Her pain is very intense now and she needs a bed. Mary wants to just crawl away and not face this. She does not have the breath to ask for His help; she just trusts that He knows. Her chest constricts more.

They come to a courtyard, and she sees Jesus in chains lying bare on the ground. Blood is everywhere. They are slashing her baby's back with whips and chains. Mary is screaming at them to stop, but no one hears her over the cheering crowds. As she takes a breath, foul odors fill her nose. The smells make her feel sick. She cannot hold it back and vomits. Mary looks up. Why did He choose her? She is not capable of this. Tears begin to roll down her cheeks. None of this feels right. How can this be part of the Father's plan? This abuse is not fit for animals; how can this be the Father's plan for His Son? Mary feels so confused. The pain around her heart is greater—tight and choking. She can no longer stand, but there are more crowds to fight.

Mary has to stay close to her baby. She tries to go to Jesus. She has to make it all better. They have now given Jesus a cross to carry. But that has been her job; she has carried all of His crosses. How can she not do it now, when Jesus needs her the most?

She cannot get to Jesus and fear sets in. The pain is getting more intense. Mary is trying to breathe through it, but there is no air to breathe in. Miles are left to go. She has to push down the pain and endure to walk on.

She continues to fight the crowds; she needs to find her baby. Finally, the crowds break, and she sees Jesus. The hammer is in the air and ready to come down. Why did He choose her? She is not capable of this. She looks away, but hears Jesus's cries. Her baby is crying out; she has to go to Him. She runs to Jesus and sees the hammer come down. She feels the hammering of the labor from long ago. It all happens so fast. How can Jesus's life be nailed away in a matter of minutes? Jesus is lifted in the air, there is a thundering pain in her chest, and Mary cannot find breath. Mary's head is groggy, her body is going numb, and her blood feels like ice, but her flesh feels on fire. The pain causes her heart to collapse, and she falls to her knees.

Is she lacking faith? All she feels right now is fear stealing her strength. She knows she has to let fear go and use her faith. Finally, she screams out, "Father!"

All seems to stop around her and there is stillness. Mary feels the Spirit come, like He did that first night.

"Daughter."

"Yahweh, please..."

"I know, you do not have to ask. I am here; I have always been here."

"I have not felt You."

"Because you are only choosing to feel your fear, and I do not dwell in fear. Finally, you broke away from it to call to Me."

"I cannot do this. Why did You choose me? I do not know how to do what You are asking of me."

"Be still, and know I am Lord. Just breathe."

"I do not know how to breathe right now. I cannot feel any breath in my lungs."

"Be still. My Spirit will be your breath."

"I need this to stop... for Him to come down... for someone to heal His wounds..."

"All you need is Me."

"This is not a righteous place for His death... He needs a holy place..."

"I am here; this is a holy place. No other place will do."

"But..."

"Daughter, stop arguing with Me. My ways are perfect, this place is perfect, and My Son is perfect. Be still, and allow Me to enter into your heart so I can accomplish My plan."

Mary becomes still and quiet, and the Holy Spirit comes upon her. Everything becomes holy. She looks around and sees the hill differently—it is sacred ground now. She looks at the cross and sees love. She looks upon her baby, and sees God.

Mary's journey with Jesus is finished. She has questioned for so long "why her," and at that cross she finally learns why... because no one is capable of being His mother but her.

LOVE'S MEMOIR

And going a little farther he fell on his face and prayed, saying, "My Father, if it be possible, let this cup pass from me; nevertheless, not as I will, but as you will."

Matthew 26:39

From noon until three in the afternoon darkness came over all the land. About three in the afternoon Jesus cried out in a loud voice, "Eli, Eli, lema sabachthani?" (which means "My God, my God, why have you forsaken me?").

Matthew 27:45-46

And being in anguish, he prayed more earnestly, and his sweat was like drops of blood falling to the ground.

Luke 22:44

So it is written: "The first man Adam became a living being"; the last Adam, a life-giving spirit.

1 Corinthians 15:45

All inhabitants of the earth will worship the beast—all whose names have not been written in the Lamb's book of life, the Lamb who was slain from the creation of the world.

Revelation 13:8

He will crush your head, and you will strike his heel.

Genesis 3:15

My God, my God, why have you forsaken me? Why are you so far from saving me, so far from my cries of anguish?

Psalm 22:19

Cleanse me with hyssop, and I will be clean.

Psalm 51:7

I will make the sun go down at noon and darken the earth in broad daylight. I will turn your religious festivals into mourning and all your singing into weeping. I will make all of you wear sackcloth and shave your heads. I will make that time like mourning for an only son and the end of it like a bitter day.

Amos 8:9-10

There is nothing but darkness, but He can still see His hands. Jesus can still see the mud that created a callous cast on His hands and arms when He created them. He remembers walking with Adam and Eve. He remembers their long talks together. He remembers the joy He would feel as He watched them discover everything new for the first time. The amazement and awe of Adam and Eve's faces as they felt the ocean waves, smelled the sweet scent of flowers, saw the beauty of a sunset, or heard the song of the birds flying high... Jesus remembers what it felt like to love them for the first time, and now that love is the only thing He can feel in this darkness.

This is not an eclipse of nature; it is deliberate. The Father turned off the light. At Jesus's birth the Father turned on the light during the darkness, and now at His Son's death the world only deserves darkness. One last time, the world will experience physical darkness. Jesus's physical suffering—the flogging, nails, thorns, mocking, and cross—are all done. Now it is time for Jesus to finish His job and absorb the darkness once and for all. It is a job of atoning, and the children will never understand. A job Jesus has been preparing for since the beginning. A plan that Jesus's heavenly body is welcoming at this moment, but His earthly body is making Him vulnerable to the pain. This has always been the plan...

The Three discussed this day at creation. Jesus remembers the moment He created the trees He is hanging on right now. The cross took two trees to make. He remembers touching the ground and they grew.[327] He made sure to grow them large and strong so they could hold His body. The hill was a lump of mud before the Father spoke to it. The Father created this hill for only this purpose. It was the only thing in creation that did not bring the Father joy. The Three walked up the hill and saw the plan. The view was beautiful from the top. The Three looked down on their creation and saw the complete story. They saw every name that was going to be uttered on the cross, and it brought Them joy. The Three knew the only time there would be true pain in the midst of the joy would be in the darkness. The Father looked to the Son, the Spirit filled the Son's lungs with breath, and all Three prepared for the darkness of the cross on that hill. The Father's plan will be complete, and everything will end with peace and joy for His children... but the darkness. The darkness. It was the darkness that the Three knew would be the greatest pain. The darkness will bring the separation of the Three. It was the darkness that Jesus prayed for His Father to take away from Him in the garden the night before.[328] The darkness will only last for three hours, but for the first time the Three will be aware of time and the hours will become eternity... [329]

---

[327] Many species of pine and spruce trees live for thousands of years; many spruce trees are recorded to be over 9,000 years old.

[328] Reference to Matthew 26:39. Jesus prayed in the garden of Gethsemane.

[329] At noon God caused the world to go dark; the light did not come back to the earth until 3:00 p.m.

Earlier in the garden, Jesus felt pure agony for the first time. His body felt weak and human. He has never been away from the Father and the Spirit and knew the moment was coming to separate. He lost control of His earthly body and broke for the first time. He was angry at the limits of His human body; words were not enough. Jesus was willing His earthly body to worship the Father, but it was not enough. He could not tell the Father enough how much He loved Him. The tears, the praise, the prayers were not enough. Jesus was trying desperately to do more, and in His determination His sweat turned into blood.[330] The pain of leaving His Father was too great. He knew the Deceiver was there with Him. He felt fear for the first time. The Deceiver filled His cup with it. Not the fear of man, but the fear of living with the Deceiver for three hours in the darkness. Three hours in all of eternity is too great for Jesus to be away from His Father and the Spirit...

Now on the cross, He is in that darkness He feared earlier. Man has never understood time. Years can go by in minutes, and minutes can turn into years. These three hours of darkness are the Son's eternity. His only comfort is to remember His children as He lets their sin wash all over Him.

He feels the betrayal of the Morning Star. He feels the sadness of Adam and Eve choosing death over life. He feels Cain's betrayal and Abel's screams. His heart breaks as the world creates idols. He feels Abraham's doubts and lies. He feels Jacob's deceit. The ten brothers sell Jesus, not Joseph, into slavery. He grows angry over the creation of slavery that will endure forever. He is frustrated over leaders losing sight of the integrity to lead. He feels disgust over David's lust. His skin burns from the furnace. He feels the disappointment of those who run away instead of following Him. He feels outrage at the world for following sin rather than His love. He hears every cry from every baby, every child that has ever been left in emptiness. He feels every broken heart,

---

[330] Luke 22:44

every loneliness, and every lie the Deceiver has ever told. He feels your sin. Your sin seeps through every pore of Jesus's broken body and fills Him with a dirty blackness that diseases Him completely. The Deceiver enters Him, and Jesus's human body screams out in pain.

The Father turns on the light again. Jesus asks for water, and a branch of hyssop with sour wine is lifted to His lips. A branch of hyssop was used a long time ago to purify; dipped in the blood of the lamb and painted on the doorframe to save souls. Now it will be used once more to purify the Lamb.

"Father, forgive them, because they do not know what they are doing."[331]

Jesus remembers David's words. He sees David on his knees, sees all of His children, crying out. He repeats the cry of their misunderstanding. Jesus shouts out the children's cry so He can now answer it.

"Eli, Eli, lema sabachthani."[332]

Jesus knows the Father has never forsaken, no matter how many times His children cry out that question to Him. The Father has always been. Jesus is now answering that question for all the children of the past, present, and future. Jesus endured the three hours, and now He is purified to finally answer that cry. The Father has never abandoned any of His children. The Father sent His Son to live through three hours of darkness because He loved them. That has always been the motivation of the plan.

"Father, I entrust My spirit into Your hands."[333]

Jesus has survived the darkness and will crush the serpent with His heel. He drinks the cup down.

"It is finished."[334]

---

[331] Luke 23:34

[332] Mark 15:34; reference to Psalm 22:1. It means "My God, my God, why have You forsaken me?"

[333] Luke 23:46

[334] John 19:30

LOVE'S PROOF

Now Thomas, one of the Twelve, was not with the disciples when Jesus came. So the other disciples told him, "We have seen the Lord!" But he said to them, "Unless I see the nail marks in his hands and put my finger where the nails were, and put my hand into his side, I will not believe." A week later his disciples were in the house again, and Thomas was with them. Though the doors were locked, Jesus came and stood among them and said, "Peace be with you!" Then he said to Thomas, "Put your finger here; see my hands. Reach out your hand and put it into my side. Stop doubting and believe." Thomas said to him, "My Lord and my God!"

John 20:24-28

My goal is that they may be encouraged in heart and united in love, so that they may have the full riches of complete understanding, in order that they may know the mystery of God, namely, Christ, in whom are hidden all the treasures of wisdom and knowledge. I tell you this so that no one may deceive you by fine-sounding arguments.

Colossians 2:2-4

Through him you believe in God, who raised him from the dead and glorified him, and so your faith and hope are in God.

1 Peter 1:21

Trust in the Lord with all your heart, and do not lean on your own under-standing. In all your ways acknowledge him, and he will make straight your paths. Be not wise in your own eyes; fear the Lord, and turn away from evil. It will be healing to your flesh and refreshment to your bones.

Proverbs 3:5-8 NKJV

Thomas stands in utter shock. He does not know if he can trust his own eyes. He does not believe it is an angel; it looks just like Jesus, but how can He be here now? Surely Jesus cannot be alive. Is He just a ghost to remind Thomas of how he abandoned Jesus at the time of His arrest?[335] Yes, that must be it, because Jesus died. Thomas looks to the others and they seem to have confidence in their eyes. He wonders if they can see something he cannot. Why can he not have blind faith like them? In Thomas's heart, Jesus is his Lord. Thomas's faith is like a twig growing into a tall, strong tree in the darkness of his heart. But in his mind, he is protecting that faith against anything the Deceiver would do to blind him. His doubts have purpose.

Just yesterday, the others tried to convince him. He felt sorry for them, for he knew their grief made their minds weak. He vowed to remain strong. They pleaded with Thomas to believe them, but he had too much respect for his faith to join them.

"I will not believe it unless I see the nail wounds in His hands, put my fingers into them, and place my hand into the wound in His side."[336]

Now Thomas is face to face with Jesus himself. Jesus does not look to the others, only at Thomas. His stare is kind, but purposeful. Jesus's only mission is Thomas. This puts fear into Thomas's heart and mind. His conviction tells Thomas that this is not a ghost of his own regret, but this is the Son in the flesh in front of him. What have his doubts brought him to?

---

[335] Thomas was among the disciples that fled at Jesus' arrest in the garden.
[336] John 20:25 NLT

Jesus looks into Thomas's heart and knows it is true to Him. A smile spreads across his face. Then He looks to all of them and says, "Peace be with you."[337]

Thomas cannot speak, he cannot think, he cannot even will his body to move at all. His whole life stops at this moment. Is this why he was chosen? Over the last several months, Thomas has agonized over why Jesus ever approached him in the first place. It was not a monumental moment; there were no miracles or grand gestures. It was just a simple conversation. It was not instant for Thomas. Simple conversations over and over again were required. Thomas would listen, and go away, and meditate on what Jesus had said. After every conversation, Thomas found himself coming back to listen some more. It was slow, but steady. Thomas needed reason and thought to make him believe and follow. Thomas had spent his whole life carefully using logic and intelligence to justify everything he did. Then he met a Man who somehow confirmed all of his rationalizations in a way that seemed contrary to everything he had ever learned or thought. When that happened, Thomas decided to follow Jesus. He was not like the others who had confidence in his heart from the beginning. He needed this Man to answer his challenges. He needed this Man to be greater than his questions. Jesus never resented or felt rejected by Thomas's needs. Jesus cherished him. Jesus would look at Thomas, as he exhausted himself in his thoughts, and smile. Jesus would think of the many conversations the Three would have about him. The pride the Three would feel every time Thomas would deeply consider which path to take.

Now standing before Thomas, Jesus knows he is not doubting Him, but doubting all the lies the world has ever told him. Thomas is not idolizing his doubts—he never has; he is just looking for the right answers. It is his response and not the way of his heart. Thomas knows his emotions are not a trustworthy foundation. Emotions are the spray

---

[337] John 20:26 NLT

of the wind; they cannot be controlled or contained, and there is no map to guide where they will go. Thomas only wants to build his house on truth and proof.[338] That will be the rock upon which he stands. That is his response to his fellow disciples—not the doubt of his Lord, but the doubt of their conjectures. Jesus understands this of Thomas's heart, and wants to give him the proof he needs because Jesus loves him so. Jesus speaks to Thomas with all the love of the Father and stretches out His hands.

"Put your fingers here and see My hands. Put your hand into the wound of My side. Do not be faithless any longer. Believe!"[339]

Was he chosen for this moment right now? Was he chosen to witness this proof? Was this the point of his entire life? Thomas looks down upon Jesus's hands and loses his breath. The weight of his body is too great for his legs and Thomas begins to collapse. The Spirit comes and lifts Thomas's body and fills his lungs with breath. Thomas focuses on the holes. They do not look bruised or bloody, but smooth and formed like they have always been there. Thomas can see through them, but oddly, the holes do not look empty.

Thomas looks to Jesus, and he knows that Jesus sees his heart. He feels loved and unworthy at the same moment. Jesus shakes His head, and Thomas knows he only needs to feel loved. Shaking, Thomas slowly approaches the Son. Thomas understands he is not confirming his faith, but touching the blueprint of God's plan in the flesh.

The holes have left flaws in Jesus's flesh. A nail cannot pierce without leaving the sewage of the sin it bared. Thomas cautiously places his fingers into the holes. He suddenly notices how dark and coarse the insides are. The flesh inside is seared with the hell of being separated from God. Thomas can feel all of God's greatness and all of the world's sin together in those holes. Tears fill his eyes, and they quickly come crashing down. He can only handle having his fingers in the

---

[338] Reference to Matthew 7:24–27.
[339] John 20:27 NLT

holes for just a moment; it is too great an experience to endure longer. Thomas is not strong enough to touch Jesus' side. In that wound, Thomas can see with his own eyes the holes sin created, and only by His scars is there grace.[340]

For so long, Thomas strove to make sense out of chaos. He has walked the straight path of protection so he would never wander. When Jesus first asked Thomas to join Him, he had doubt then. Thomas lacked the confidence to be certain of Jesus's truth. Then Thomas became cautious. No more doubt, but he was careful to avoid risk. Like a slow drip, the cautiousness turned into analytical reasoning. Thomas used logic to collect all of his information on Jesus. Now the Son is in front of Thomas asking him to accept the divine. The Son is asking him to perceive the Son intuitively, without conscious reasoning, just instinct. Instinct to see and accept the supreme good of Jesus standing before him. No more asking why, no more wondering about the plan, and no more relying on self.

Those holy "scars Jesus bore are not incidental but fundamental. Jesus, who came to heal, chose to keep His scars and carry them to Heaven." Thomas knows those scars will be the only evidence of man in heaven.[341]

Thomas looks back to Jesus and breathlessly exclaims, "My Lord and my God!"[342]

Doubt has proven love.

---

[340] Jesus showed His scars from the crucifixion to others after His resurrection. The Bible refers to Him as still carrying the scars on His heavenly body in Luke 24:39-40; John 20:20, 27; Revelation 5:6, 12.

[341] From the notes of Pastor Todd Peters.

[342] John 20:28 NLT

LOVE'S ATONEMENT

The Jewish leaders were infuriated by Stephen's accusation, and they shook their fists at him in rage. But Stephen, full of the Holy Spirit, gazed steadily into heaven and saw the glory of God, and he saw Jesus standing in the place of honor at God's right hand. And he told them, "Look, I see the heavens opened and the Son of Man standing in the place of honor at God's right hand!" Then they put their hands over their ears and began shouting. They rushed at him and dragged him out of the city and began to stone him. His accusers took off their coats and laid them at the feet of a young man named Saul. As they stoned him, Stephen prayed, "Lord Jesus, receive my spirit." He fell to his knees, shouting, "Lord, don't charge them with this sin!" And with that, he died... Saul was one of the witnesses, and he agreed completely with the killing of Stephen... Saul was going everywhere to destroy the church. He went from house to house, dragging out both men and women to throw them into prison.

Acts 7:54-8:1-3 NLT

And lest I should be exalted above measure through the abundance of the revelations, there was given to me a thorn in the flesh, the messenger of Satan to buffet me, lest I should be exalted above measure. For this thing I besought the Lord thrice, that it might depart from me. And he said unto me, "My grace is sufficient for thee: for my strength is made perfect in weakness." Most *gladly therefore will I rather glory in my infirmities, that the power of Christ may rest upon me. Therefore, I take pleasure in infirmities, in reproaches, in necessities, in persecutions, in distresses for Christ's sake: for when I am weak, then am I strong.*

2 Corinthians 12:7-10 NKJV

Then some Jews came from Antioch and Iconium and won the crowd over. They stoned Paul and dragged him outside the city, thinking he was dead. But after... he got up and went back into the city...

Acts 14:19-20

The name of the Lord is a fortified tower; the righteous run to it and are safe.

Proverbs 18:10

I have loved you with an everlasting love; I have drawn you with unfailing kindness. I will build you up again.

Jeremiah 31:3-4

The high council is assembling, and they have already determined Stephen's guilt before he speaks. Their questions show their lack of understanding of God's plan. Stephen's testimony falls onto deaf ears, enraging his judges. Stephen knows there is no argument to make; he rests in the truth, and becomes silent. His silence angers his accusers more, and they begin to hail down their fury upon him. The Spirit comes and intercedes.[343] Stephen hears nothing but the Spirit's words.

"Stephen, you are a man full of faith, and I will fill you now."

The Spirit breathes out, and Stephen breathes in.

"Stephen, look up. I will reveal My glory to you."

---

[343] Reference to Acts 7:54-55.

The Spirit opens his eyes, and Stephen can see heaven. There, he sees the glory of God and Jesus standing in the place of honor at God's right hand.[344] It is more beautiful than Stephen ever could have imagined.

"Look, I see the heavens open and the Son of Man standing in the place of honor at God's right hand!"[345]

Stephen shouts this in joy to the crowd, never taking his eyes off of Jesus. All he can see is the glory. Stephen does not feel the first rock. Tears fill his eyes and begin to flow as the Spirit fills him with joy. Stephen does not feel the second rock; his smile just gets bigger. Stephen does not feel the third rock, nor the one that strikes the side of his head.[346] The Spirit is there covering him, and all Stephen can feel is His love holding him. Stephen's joy overtakes his soul, and a song of praise bursts out. Stephen sees the Father and Son smiling at him, and he does not feel the next rock crash against his mouth as he sings. All Stephen can do is fill the air with songs of praise to the Lord.

The accusers drag Stephen out of the city and the stoning escalates. The official witnesses take off their coats and lay them at the feet of a young man in charge of the scene. The young man who shouts the loudest, carrying the most hate in his heart, is a man named Saul.[347] Stephen locks eyes on Saul and does not break the stare. In the midst of the blood and broken bones, a smile forms on his lips. The stare becomes determined and focused. Saul becomes uncomfortable, but Stephen does not let him look away. Then Stephen speaks to the Father but does not break his stare from Saul.

"Lord Jesus, receive my spirit."[348]

Stephen falls to his knees, but continues to look at Saul.

"Lord, do not charge them with this sin."[349]

---

[344] Reference to Acts 7:56.

[345] Acts 7:56

[346] Reference to Acts 7:57-58.

[347] Reference to Acts 7:58.

[348] Acts 7:59

[349] Acts 7:60

Saul feels his soul jump, and he wants to run away but cannot. Stephen does not feel the next rock. It hits him straight on his forehead, and blood pours down his face. Stephen's body comes crashing down into the dirt. Stephen dies, but his smile is still there...

Paul jumps out of unconsciousness. He is covered in sweat. Paul is confused; he cannot remember how he came to this place. The only thing Paul can remember is his dream just now. It is always the same dream; a memory that has become his life's nightmare. No matter the circumstances, when Paul closes his eyes, the dream hunts him as if it happened yesterday. Stephen's words still echo in his ears. He remembers every moment from that day, even how the dust of the ground tasted in his mouth the moment Stephen fell onto it in his death. He can still smell the blood in the air. He can still hear the shouts of the crowd. He will never forget how Stephen stared at him as the rocks decimated his body. His nightmare always ends with that stare.

The dream always makes Paul's head hurt. This time it has made his head throb more than usual. Paul raises his hands to cradle his aching mind and feels a warm wetness. He looks at his hands and sees blood. For a moment, he thinks the dream came to life and it is Stephen's blood to plague him, but then he remembers that happened almost fifteen years ago. He notices that he has blood all over him, and then he feels the pain. His whole body feels broken, and the memories of the rocks being hurled at him come flooding back. He has been stoned.[350] Suddenly his body feels weak, and he lies down again.

Paul begins to take inventory of his injuries. He tastes blood inside his mouth, and looking up through his swollen eyes, he whispers, "Please take this from me... Please take this thorn."

He has wished it in his heart a million times, but has only asked for it two other times before. Now for the third time, Paul is asking the

---

[350] Theologians believed Paul's stoning happened about fifteen years after Stephen's death.

Lord to take it away from him.[351] It is a thorn that has pierced his side for too long. A thorn he can no longer bear.

Every time he makes progress, every time he feels the Spirit move, that is when the Deceiver twists the thorn into his side more. For years, Paul believed he deserved the burden of this cross and never asked for it to be lifted. He needed his guilt; it fulfilled him. Without his guilt who was he? It is the thorn that keeps him humble, it is the thorn that keeps him motivated, and it is the thorn that makes him love. The thorn is for his own good. That is what he convinced himself to believe for years. But lately, with every step, the thorn is causing him to stumble more and more.[352]

Paul knows now it is not God's plan for him to carry this thorn, but Satan is repeatedly crushing him over and over with it. He comes as a messenger and whispers in Paul's ear that he will never be more than his guilt. It is Satan who is causing Paul to have an infirmity of inadequacy. A thorn sent by Satan to continually remind Paul that he will never be justified from his guilt.[353] A thorn from Satan saying he will never be more than Saul.

Paul's stoning has finally helped him understand Stephen's experience. Paul is now ready to allow God to remove this thorn...

The first time he asked God to take it away, the Father responded by saying, "My grace is sufficient for you."[354]

Paul tried to let that be enough, but it was not.

"Yes, Lord, Your grace is always enough for me... *but...*"

Satan knows Paul is not ready to relinquish control to God; there is still room in Paul's heart for the Deceiver to twist the thorn.

The second time Paul sought the Lord, he was weak and could no longer carry the shame, so he got on his knees.

---

[351] The Bible states that Paul prayed to God a total of three times to take away his "thorn."

[352] Many theologians believe Paul's "thorn" was not a physical, but an emotional problem. Paul's own remembrance of his past was his thorn; Paul's past included the persecution of the church (Acts 8:1-3; Gal. 1:13; Phil 3:6).

[353] Paul states that his "thorn" is sent as a messenger from Satan.

[354] 2 Corinthians 12:9

"Lord, please take this thorn from me."

"My grace is sufficient for you."

"Yes, Lord, *but* if You could just do this one thing for me..."

Satan smiles; he still has a place in Paul's heart...

Now Paul has been left for dead. Some probably thought he was already dead. The stones hit him hard, and this time he believes it to be his end too. He is at peace with it, for he is so exhausted. It is not the stoning, prison, shipwrecks, or any other trial he has gone through, but it is the thorn he no longer has the strength left to fight. There has never been a pain greater than the pain of his own actions as Saul.[355] Saul was the thorn. The Deceiver knows that and reminds him of his past every time he begins to feel like Paul. As he feels like he is surely dying, Paul asks God to take this thorn away from him one last time. He lies there and waits.

"My Father, come to me and hear me. For years, I did not have the strength or courage to speak my own confession to You. My ears could not hear the confession of all my sins. Now, as I lie here about to die, I confess to You... I confess Saul. Please, Father, take this thorn before I die."

The Spirit comes to Paul and lies next to him.

"My grace is sufficient for you."

Paul is finally ready to understand.

"I thought I understood that, but I did not. I have believed in Your grace; I have preached it to all who can hear, but it has not been enough for me because I still see Saul in my reflection. Why will You not take Saul away?"

"Why do you not trust My grace?"

"I do. I have given You everything I am."

"No, you have not."

"What else do I have to give? I am lying here dying because I have given all of myself for Your plan. You are all that I love and serve."

---

[355] Paul's original Jewish name was Saul. He changed it to Paul once he became a believer in Jesus Christ.

"No. You are serving yourself first."

"How can You say that? I do not want anything for myself—just You."

"Then why is there guilt in your heart?"

"I do not know. Why have You not taken it away from me?"

"The Son did take it away. He nailed it to the cross. Guilt is from the Deceiver, not Me. Shame and guilt have been your idol. If I were in your heart completely there would be no room for guilt. If you trusted that My grace was enough, then Saul would leave. I have taken every pain away on the cross, but you have to trust in that, and you have not. That is why you still have a thorn in your flesh."

"What should I do?"

"Allow My power to rest on you. Allow Me to make you strong. Allow My grace to be sufficient for you."

Paul begins to cry. All of these years have not been about the thorn keeping him humble to do God's work, but instead, the thorn has been there to help humble him to accept God's grace. Paul cannot be exalted until he has accepted the grace of the cross to take away his thorn. Satan has tried to use this thorn to prevent Paul from giving control to God, and the Devil has succeeded time and time again. But now, Paul is finally ready to let go of Saul. With little breath left in his lungs, Paul whispers, "Lord, forgive me."

"Trust Me to remove the thorn, and give Me your whole heart."

"Yes. Your grace is sufficient for me."

The thorn is gone. Satan has left; there is no more room left in Paul's heart. The Spirit enters into his body, and Paul can no longer feel the pain from the stones. The Spirit fills his lungs with new breath. Paul gathers himself and stands, and begins to walk back to the city.[356] Paul knows he will never feel the pain of the thorn again.

---

[356] Paul was in Iconium preaching when he was dragged out of the city to be stoned. The next day he left with Barnabas for the city Derbe.

LOVE'S EDEN

I, John, your brother and companion in the suffering and kingdom and patient endurance that are ours in Jesus, was on the island of Patmos because of the word of God and the testimony of Jesus. On the Lord's Day I was in the Spirit, and I heard behind me a loud voice like a trumpet, which said: "Write on a scroll what you see and send it to the seven churches: to Ephesus, Smyrna, Pergamum, Thyatira, Sardis, Philadelphia and Laodicea."

Revelation 1:9-11

In the beginning God created the heavens and the earth... Now the Lord God had planted a garden in the east, in Eden; and there he put the man he had formed... So the Lord God banished him from the Garden of Eden to work the ground from which he had been taken. After he drove the man out, he placed on the east side of the Garden of Eden cherubim and a flaming sword flashing back and forth to guard the way to the tree of life.

Genesis 1:1, 2:8, 3:23-24

Then the angel showed me the river of the water of life, as clear as crystal, flowing from the throne of God and of the Lamb down the middle of the great street of the city. On each side of the river stood the tree of life, bearing twelve crops of fruit, yielding its fruit every month. And the leaves of the tree are for the healing of the nations. No longer will there be any curse. The *throne of God and of the Lamb will be in the city, and his servants will serve him. They will see his face, and his name will be on their foreheads. There will be no more night. They will not need the light of a lamp or the light of the sun, for the Lord God will give them light. And they will reign for ever and ever... I am the Alpha and the Omega, the First and the Last, the Beginning and the End... The grace of the Lord Jesus be with God's people. Amen.*

Revelation 22:1-5, 13, 21

"I am the Alpha and the Omega," says the Lord God, who is, and who was, and who is to come, the Almighty.

Revelation 1:8

It is a prison. A thirty-square-mile prison. Patmos Island. Only the lowest of the low are sent here: Rome's despised vermin. An island with nothing but desolation and emptiness left from the volcano that has dictated its landscape. No trees or lush grass, just leftover rocks and debris of a burning hell. Isolated, without escape—the island's only purpose is to break the prisoners who are left to work in the mines all day.[357] Labor so great, it euthanizes the old and cripples the young. Patmos is an island created to kill.[358]

It has been ten years. Three thousand, six hundred, and fifty days on this island for John. A place that is sterile and unable to produce any living thing has become John's Revelation of God's plan. John never feels lonely, for he has the company of millions of angels and the Spirit. Toiling that was supposed to kill him only causes him to be stronger in his old age.[359] Yahweh sent John here to finish the story.

---

[357] Patmos was a copper mining island. Prisoners were forced to work in the mines.
[358] Patmos means "my killing."
[359] Historians believe John was in his late eighties to early nineties while he was on the island.

John will be the last author. Thirty-four have come before him, all together through the Spirit to write a masterpiece.[360] To write the greatest love story ever told. Now Yahweh brought John to this island to finish. Ten years of writing. Ten years of discovering a new love. Ten years of discovering a new hope. A revelation of hope for the Father's children.

After twelve hours of labor, the Father fills John with visions of blessings, and John can only feel the energy of God's glory.[361] Therefore, John writes.

"God blesses the one who reads the words of this prophecy... and He blesses all who listen to its message and obeys what it says... Grace and peace to you from the One Who is, Who always was, and Who is still to come... and from Jesus Christ. He is the... ruler of all the kings of the world. All glory to Him who loves us and has freed us from our sins by shedding His blood for us... When I saw Him, I fell at His feet... but He laid His right hand on me and said, 'Do not be afraid! I am the Alpha and the Omega; the first and the last... And I hold the keys of death and grave.'"[362]

With his lungs full of the dust of the caves, John breathes out a story for the children to understand the plan. It began in a garden. A beautiful, perfect world full of love, and then the darkness entered. All was separated. His children set out on a quest to leave the Father and find their own way without Him. The Father's heart broke, and has been breaking over and over again, looking for His lost children. The Father has to call them back to Him and provide a plan of rescue. John writes on...

"I have this complaint against you. You do not love Me, or each other, as you did at first! Look how far you have fallen! Turn back to

---

[360] There were a total of thirty-five authors who penned the Bible through the guidance of the Holy Spirit.

[361] Prisoners on the island did shifts of at least twelve hours of labor in the mines.

[362] Revelation 1:3–18 NLT

Me... Anyone with ears to hear, must listen to the Spirit and understand... to everyone who is victorious I will give fruit from the tree of
life in the paradise of God."[363]

John sits crouched; he can no longer straighten his back—a symp-
tom from contorting his body while digging. He does not feel the pain,
but only the pain the children have created in the world instead. The
children have built high walls, and they cannot reach the Father any
longer. All the children can see or feel is the pain. John writes...

"I know about your suffering and your poverty... Do not be afraid
of what you are about to suffer. The devil will throw some of you into
prison to test you... But if you remain faithful even when facing death,
I will give you the crown of life... Anyone with ears to hear must listen
to the Spirit and understand what He is saying..."[364]

With his eyes knowing nothing but the darkness of the tunnels,
John can only see God's glorious light. John writes of the tragedy
of living in the cold shadow of death that comes with the darkness.
John writes...

"You have a reputation for being alive—but you are dead. Wake
up! Strengthen what little remains, for even what is left is almost dead.
I find that your actions do not meet the requirements of my God. Go
back to what you heard and believed at first; hold to it firmly. Repent
and turn to Me again..."[365]

Ingesting poison day after day from the mines, John only feels the
pure, clean truth of God's Word throughout his body. He prays for those
infested with poison from the Deceiver. John continues to write...

"Yet there are some... who have not soiled their clothes with evil.
They will walk with Me in white, for they are worthy... I will never
erase their names from the Book of Life, but I will announce before my
Father and His angels that they are mine... What He opens, no one can

---

[363] Revelation 2:4-7 NLT
[364] Revelation 2:9-11 NLT
[365] Revelation 3:1-3 NLT

close; and what He closes, no one can open... I have opened a door for you that no one can close. You have little strength, yet you obeyed My word and did not deny Me... I am coming soon. Hold on to what you have, so that no one will take away your crown. All who are victorious will become... citizens in the city of My God... Anyone with ears to hear must listen to the Spirit..."[366]

Ten years of labor have left a lifetime of scars on John's hands. The arthritis of his toiling has turned his hands into a crippled powerhouse for God's words. John looks at his hands and wonders, "Why him?" Why is he chosen to write the Spirit's end? John's hands ache from the pressure, but he knows the children must hear. John lifts the pen again. John writes...

"Here I am! I stand at the door and knock. If anyone hears My voice and opens the door, I will come in and eat with that person, and they with Me. To the one who is victorious, I will give the right to sit with Me on My throne, just as I was victorious and sat down with My Father on His throne. Whoever has ears, let them hear what the Spirit says..."[367]

John's old body becomes alive with the excitement of the glory of it all. He prays for the Spirit to guide his pen. John writes...

"'Worthy is the Lamb, who was slain, to receive... honor and glory and praise!' Then I heard every creature in heaven and on earth and under the earth and on the sea... saying, 'To Him who sits on the throne and to the Lamb be praise and honor and glory and power, for ever and ever!'[368] 'Great and marvelous are Your deeds, Lord God Almighty, just and true are Your ways, King of the nations. Who will not fear You, Lord, and bring glory to Your name for You alone are holy... for Your righteous acts have been revealed.'"[369]

---

[366] Revelation 3:4–13 NLT
[367] Revelation 3:20–22
[368] Revelation 5:12–14
[369] Revelation 15:3–4

John looks to the sky, and the Spirit shows him the end of the plan. How can he write such a supernatural finale? There are not human words to describe God's holiness, but the Spirit gives him a way. John writes...

"Then I saw an angel coming down from heaven... He seized the dragon—that old serpent, who is the devil, Satan... The angel threw him into the bottomless pit, which He then shut and locked so Satan could not deceive the nations anymore... [370] I heard a loud shout from the throne, saying, 'Look, God's home is now among his people! He will live with them, and they will be His people. God Himself will be with them. He will wipe every tear from their eyes, and there will be no more death or sorrow or crying or pain. All these things are gone forever.' And the One sitting on the throne said, 'Look, I am making everything new!'... He also said, 'It is finished! I am the Alpha and the Omega—the Beginning and the End. To all who are thirsty I will give freely from the springs of the water of life. All who are victorious will inherit all these blessings, and I will be their God, and they will be My children...'[371]

"The city has no need of sun or moon, for the glory of God illuminates the city, and the Lamb is its light... Nothing evil will be allowed to enter... but only those whose names are written in the Lamb's book of life.[372]... No longer will there be a curse upon anything. For the throne of God and of the Lamb will be there, and His servants will worship Him. And they will see His face, and His name will be written on their foreheads... the Lord God will shine on them. And they will reign forever and ever."[373]

John finishes the story. Ten years have gone by. It has taken ten years to write the proper conclusion. Since the beginning, the children have

---

[370] Revelation 20:1-3 NLT
[371] Revelation 21:1-7
[372] Revelation 21:22-27
[373] Revelation 22:1-5

not understood how love can come from pain. Why did the Father ever allow pain to enter? That has been the children's cry from the beginning. The children have never seen the love story in the pain, but it has always been there. Every time a child cried "why me," or questioned the plan, and did not have the breath to take another step, the love was there.

It began with the Father's breath—molding and molding everything you are. Your beginning started with His love. The Father wanted you. The Father created a whole world for you to explore. The Father created it from His love. The Father did not create the path of pain, but is guiding you through it safely. The Father gives you breath before each step, and goes before you because of His love. The Father is writing a love story for you. John rejoices in this truth as he looks out upon his home of ten years.

It took the island of Patmos for John to find his love story ending. It took the long days, labor, broken bones, and ten years of toxic venom in his life to fully see the glory of the Father's Revelation. Good does not come from evil—there will not be a time when the children will see the good from the pain of the devil. But the Revelation is coming... when the pain comes, the children will see the good of the Father. The Father, in all of His triumph, will come with horns blaring to set the pain right. His good will be greater than the pain. His good will come in thundering shouts or peaceful whispers, but it will come always. It will come quick like a thief in the night or slowly like dripping dew, but it will come. The Revelation is... the Father will give His breath to His children when the pain leaves them breathless. The Revelation is... the Father's plan will never be sidetracked from the pain. The Revelation is... the Father will answer every cry with His love.

John is the last one of the followers.[374] The last one of Jesus's friends. John thinks of his friend on the cross. At the time, John

---

[374] John was the last living apostle at this time.

cursed that he was among the ones to witness the horror. Now he feels so honored the Father chose him to be there to see the beauty of it all. The Father has chosen him to witness miracles and the history of all mankind. He has walked along a path of turmoil and of righteousness. The Father gave John story after story to build his life upon. Now the Father chooses him to be the final author. In His great wisdom, the Father places John on this desolate island for His greatest story yet. John smiles and looks out onto the home he has been blessed to live on for the last ten years. He looks out onto his Eden and praises the Father.

LOVE'S EPILOGUE

He broke my strength in midlife, cutting short my days. But I cried to Him, O my God, who lives forever, don't take my life while I am so young!

Psalm 102:23-24 NLT

For by grace, you have been saved through faith, and that not of yourselves; it is the gift of God, not of works, lest anyone should boast. For we are His workmanship, created in Christ Jesus for good works, which God prepared beforehand that we should walk in them.

Ephesians 2:8-10

For I am convinced that neither death nor life, neither angels nor demons, neither the present nor the future, nor any powers, neither height nor depth, nor anything else in all creation, will be able to separate us from the love of God that is in Christ Jesus our Lord.

Romans 8:38-39

I have fought the good fight, I have finished the race, I have kept the faith. Finally, there is laid up for me the crown of righteousness, which the Lord, the righteous Judge, will give to me on that Day...

2 Timothy 4:7-8

He is frantically rummaging around through the darkness. He cannot remember how he entered this darkness. He cannot see anything; he moves his hands around like a blind man searching for something to grasp onto. He is a son; a boy just entering manhood. Too young to feel secure, but too old to feel helpless. In the distance he notices a faint light. He blinks his eyes trying to focus on the light, but his eyes are struggling to adjust to it. The light begins to grow larger and comes closer to him. He feels warmth from it. Then he hears his name being called, but he cannot find the direction the voice is coming from. The voice does not seem to be coming from one particular direction, but it encompasses every inch of the darkness. He knows who the voice belongs to. A child knows his parent's voice even in darkness.

"God is that You? God... God I cannot see anything. I'm scared. What is happening?"

"Be still. I Am here."

The voice is not loud and thundering, but soft and gentle. The Spirit holds the son, and he begins to feel calm. He still does not understand where he is, but sorrow immediately enters his spirit. He can feel a coldness filling his body.

"My feet are cold."

"Yes, I know."

The son does not understand why, but a sudden feeling of remorse overcomes him.

"God, I feel so confused."

"Yes, I know."

The coldness is numbing his toes.

"It's so dark. Why can't I see You?"

"Your eyes will adjust when it is time."

The word "time" echoes in the son's ears. Like an epiphany, he realizes that time is a misconception. He has tried to control it, but he understands now. The son understands why his feet feel so cold. Chaos constrains his emotions, and he feels out of control. The son helplessly grasps around the darkness, naively thinking something will help him to balance this situation. He is like a drowning man trying to hold onto the waves to keep from going under, but the waves only crash down on him instead of being his savior.

"How much time is left?"

"Not much. Soon this will be done."

"Will it hurt?"

"No, I Am here with you."

The son wants that to comfort him, but it does not.

"How did I get here? What happened?"

"Why does it matter? The 'why' never matters; all that matters is that you are here with Me."

This is not how the son thought his time would be spent. He thought he had all the time in the world—how did it all go so quickly? The son remembers it all in a flash. Pictures of beautiful joy and happiness play before him like a movie. He sees all the moments he was too blinded to recognize before. He realizes that he allowed so many things to blind him: pain, shame, choices, and lies from the Deceiver that told him he was never good enough. Too many beautiful moments were stolen from him, and not seeing the truth before is causing the deepest regret in his heart now.

"I've made so many wrong choices. I'm so ashamed. I do not deserve to be here with You now."

"Why?"

"You have always kept Your promises to me, and I was supposed to do my part in serving and pleasing You. I failed. I could have done better."

"Could you?"

"Yes. I allowed the world to have its way with me. I did not want to; it all happened so fast. I was walking along the path correctly, and for just a moment I turned away. It was only for a moment, but then when I turned back to the path, I couldn't see it anymore. I thought I was going in the right direction, but I wasn't."

The Spirit holds the son tighter, and the Father looks upon him with such pride and love in His heart. The Father has heard this repentance from all of His children.

"Yes, you stumbled, but no more than all of My children. What you see as boulders in your path, I see as just pebbles. They never kept you from Me. You kept Me in your heart, and that is all that matters."

"But I did not keep You in my mind always. I stopped looking at You. I was blinded by everything else. Please forgive me for being blinded."

"Many get blinded, but you never stopped looking at Me. If so, I would not be here with you now."

The coldness is entering his legs. It is reaching up to his knees. The son suddenly has a new revelation, and he begins to shake.

"Wait... I have to tell everyone... I have to tell everyone..."

"There is nothing you have to say."

"Yes, I have to tell them goodbye."

"No, this is not goodbye."

"But they're going to have pain."

"Shhh... be still."

"But what about their pain?"

"I have known about their pain since the beginning. I have been preparing to heal them for a long time... but 'I consider that the sufferings of this present time are not worth comparing with the glory that is to be revealed' to them."[375]

"But I cannot let this be my testimony. I thought the plan for my life would be different. I haven't done anything in life to define me yet. I wanted so much more for my life. Now all I am left with is this regret. I wanted to be special and do something important... didn't You plan more for me than this?"

He feels a heavy pressure in his chest. The pressure is slowing his breath, and the coldness is to his waist now.

"What do you know of My plans?"

---

[375] Romans 8:18

He feels ashamed. "I don't. I just thought You would have a plan for me beyond this."

The coldness is moving faster now—it is reaching his chest.

"God, I can't stand this regret. What have I done? Bad choices, doubt, and loneliness have defined me."

"Son, I define you. Only Me. Does anyone else know how you were knitted in the womb?[376] Does anyone else know the hairs on your head?[377] Does anyone else know how I created your smile? Does anyone else know the number of tears you have cried? No, only Me. Only I have known you every moment of your life. I define you. You are My testimony of a masterpiece that I created with love."

The Father sees the son still has doubts. He makes His light grow bigger and His voice louder.

"Son, don't you see I have waited thousands of years for this moment right now? For the moment I can have you all to Myself. Away from the world. I have been writing stories for thousands of years for you so you could know Me and choose Me. I created the world and I have been making it continue on day after day for thousands of years... making the sun and moon rise, the seasons come and go... so time would continue long enough for you to be born. It has all been for you because that is how much I have longed to have you as My son. Only one plan has ever mattered: My plan. Man's plan is selfish and shortsighted. My plan was never to give you to the world, but to give the world to you. You wanted a plan for your life to make you feel like you matter, but My plan of rescuing you with My love is what makes you matter... nothing you could have done in your life is bigger than that plan. This is why I have been writing this story... I wanted you to know Me and love Me, so I then can love you. It was all for this moment; you are the child I have planned for all along. This whole plan has been for you."

---

[376] Reference to Psalm 139:13-14.
[377] Reference to Luke 12:7.

"Why? I'm so unworthy of Your love. I have tried over and over again to kill the sin inside of me, but I always failed."

The coldness takes hold of his shoulders.

"If you failed then I would not be here now. Your sin was never intended for you to kill. I did not create you to be strong enough to endure it without Me. You were created to only rest on Me, and when resolution was needed, I gave My Son, Jesus. I wanted this moment with you so much that I allowed Him to be on that cross so you could be with Me now. Jesus spoke your name out on the cross and it's all finished... He killed your sin. Do not look back any longer. My sweet son, I have always known your heart. You are here with Me now because you always kept your heart filled with love for Me. Even in the times when your mind was not thinking of Me, your heart never wavered."

The coldness flows down his arms to his fingers.

"Is this the end? Is this my story?"

"What is wrong with this story?"

"It feels incomplete. I did not have enough time to do more."

"I've been writing lots of stories for a long time, and no one thinks there was ever enough time. My children only focus on the time instead of the glory in their story. All of My children only see the pain, trials, or the tears. They do not understand what I see. What makes a life complete? Who judges when time is enough? Who created time? Who knows the beginning, middle, and end? Who is the author of every life that has ever lived? All of My stories end with love for those who know Me. From My first son, Adam, to you now, I have only rescued and loved My children. Stories are not complete because of works and deeds your feeble human hands can achieve, but are completed when My glory is achieved. Once that happens in a life, it is time for My child to come home to Me."

"I achieved Your glory?"

"Yes."

The coldness starts to go up his neck.

"Will everyone left behind understand that?"

"No. They will focus on the pain. But just like your story, their story will not end with the pain. I will rescue them too. Someday 'I will wipe away every tear from their eyes, and death shall be no more, neither shall there be mourning, nor crying, nor pain anymore, for the former things have passed away.' Someday all of My children will understand My plan. They will know glory is not in their earthly plans, but only in Me."[378]

"Will you give them answers? That's all I ever wanted... just to know the answers."

"You never trusted Me to show them to you."

"I know. I am sorry."

"What answer do you want to know?"

The son knows the question that has tormented his soul for so long, but he is too scared to utter the words. It is the same question that has haunted all of God's children since the beginning. Adam... David... Paul... they all asked it. The Spirit's light grows brighter. The coldness is in his head now, but he no longer feels it.

"I know your question. Look into My hands now and you will see all of the answers."

The coldness stops. Everything stops. The son lets out a long, slow breath and then he stops. The Spirit then breathes into the son's nostrils His breath, and the son exhales his first breath. It tastes sweet and pure. His eyes finally adjust, and he can see the Father. The Father's beauty overwhelms the son.

The son carefully approaches the Father and looks down into His hands. There, the son sees everything. Every doubt, question, and need is answered. He looks up to his Father and whispers the answer...

"Everything will be alright; the Lord loves me."[379]

The Father smiles with pride, and embraces His son.

"Let's go home."

---

[378] Revelation 21:4
[379] Quote from the journal of Colton Repp.